St. Croix Island Travel Guide, USVI

Vacation, Holiday, Honeymoon

Author

Williams Barnes

Copyright Notice

Table of Content

Introduction 1

History 3

Tourism... 11

Traveling Information 15

Accommodations 21

Nightlife... 26

Restaurants 27

Shopping 30

Transportation 34

    Air Travel 37

    Car Rentals 41

    Taxis & Rates 42

    Sailing and Boating 56

Activities Guide... 62

    Scuba Diving 67

    Charter Boats... 71

      Virgin Islands: Fishing Guide (This is Virgin Island
Fishing Guide related to all Virgin Islands) 75

      Virgin Islands: Fishing Regulations (This is Virgin Island
Fishing Regulations related to all Virgin Islands) 85

    Golf & Tennis 92

    Virgin Islands Culture (This is Virgin Island Culture related
to all Virgin Islands) 95

      Virgin Islands Language 99

      Virgin Islands People................................... 108

      Virgin Islands Music 113

      Virgin Islands Food & Drinks....................... 116

Attractions guide... 123

    Christiansted, St. Croix 125

    Frederiksted, St. Croix 131

    Nature Reserves on St. Croix 134

Beaches 137

Wedding Planning *153*
Real Estate *158*

Introduction

About St. Croix

Three National Parks: Salt River which protects a diverse ecosystem in addition to pre-historic ruins; Buck Island with stunning marine gardens; and five historic structures in Christiansted that give visitors a look into Danish colonial way of life. Additional parks and preserves include: Sandy Point notable for its beauty and for its protected sea turtles, and Jack and Isaac Bays.

St. Croix was once the sugar producing king of the Caribbean. Today visitors will note dozens of sugar mill ruins scattered across the island; there are around 150.

Visitors can learn about this important part of USVI history by visiting historic sites such as Whim Plantation, a restored and preserved sugar plantation.

"The Wall", if you are a diver you have likely heard of it! St. Croix is well known for wonderful dive opportunities. If you aren't a diver you can take introductory classes while on vacation. Additional water sports your vacation to St. Croix might include are snorkeling, kayaking, fishing and boating. On land you can plan a game of golf, take an island tour, explore scenic forests by jeep, enjoy jazz at outdoor concerts, shop, dine, catch a crab race at a local bar, or a horse race at the track.

You can fly directly to St. Croix, it has an airport. Taking a daytrip or better yet an overnight visit to St. Croix from St. Thomas is made possible by regular interisland air service and a ferry.

History

The last of the Native Indian people to inhabit St. Croix were the Carib. Originally from the Guiana region of South America, the Carib people were not the first Indians on St. Croix. They had gained presence of the islands from the Tainos or Arawaks in the early 1400's. It was however the Carib that greeted Columbus on his second voyage through the islands.

Christopher Columbus

Christopher Columbus visited St. Croix on November 14th, 1493 on his second voyage to the New World. Columbus named the island Santa Cruz (Holy Cross). The explorers anchored off a natural bay west of

Christiansted, known today as Salt River. Some two-dozen armed men from Columbus' fleet went ashore to explore. These men were met by defensive arrows to which they retreated. The Salt River site is the first and only positively documented site associated with Columbus' exploration of the New World on what is today a U.S. territory.

The Caribs continued their existence on St. Croix for about a decade following Columbus' visit. During this period they had established an understanding of mutual coexistence with the Spanish on Puerto Rico. This understanding was concluded when a Spanish adventurer raided St. Croix for Carib slaves. The Caribs joined in an effort with the Tainos of Puerto Rico, against the Spanish. For their uprising they were condemned to be destroyed by the Spanish Crown. With 'legalized' extermination and military action imminent the Caribs permanently abandoned St. Croix.

Although Columbus landed on Croix in the name of Spain, the first to establish themselves on St. Croix were the Dutch and English with a small number of French Protestants. In 1625 both countries, Britain and the Netherlands, co-existed on the island. This mutually beneficial relationship of sharing St. Croix ended without question when the islands Dutch governor killed the English counterpart. The English retaliated, leaving the Dutch governor dead. Many years of battles over possession of the island followed between the two powers.

Dutch and French settlers slowly retreated leaving the English in power of St. Croix. The colony grew under British rule. The Spanish, on nearby Puerto Rico, were concerned by the growth. In a surprise attack the Spanish landed on St. Croix and killed many settlers and forced the others to leave. The French heard of the overthrow of the English and took the opportunity to move in themselves and take over St. Croix from the

Spanish. This was around 1650. Philippe de Poincy, an official of the Knights of Malta, sent 160 of his best troops to capture St. Croix. He succeeded and then quickly sent some three hundred planters from St. Kitts to establish settlements on the newly captured colony.

French West India Company

Seeking to establish a stronger hold on St. Croix, Louis XIV decided that the French Crown should take over. In 1665 the French West India Company was formed and sent to St. Croix. The Company rule did not do very well and lasted only seven years. The King dissolved the Company and replaced it with Crown rule. The French Crown continued to claim ownership of St. Croix although they had basically abandoned the island. Most of the French settlers had left the island by 1695.

Danish West Indies Company

On June 13,1733 the Danish West Indies Company bought the island from France. The Danish West Indian

Company wasted no time in sending settlers to St. Croix to form their new colony. Under the leadership of Frederik Moth, a new town at Christiansted was planned within the first year.

In 1747, St. Croix was given its own government, separate from St. Thomas and St. John. Under strict regulations, the planters soon became frustrated with company rule. In 1753 the planters of the three islands petitioned the King to buy out the company. In 1754 the islands became a royal colony. With the crown directly involved a long period of growth followed. The Crown designated the most lucrative of the islands – St. Croix – as the new capital for all three islands. Thus, the capital of St. Thomas and St. John was moved from Charlotte Amalie on St. Thomas to Christiansted where it remained until 1871 when it was returned to Charlotte Amalie.

Sugar

For some time St. Croix was one of the wealthiest islands in the West Indies. The prosperity was due greatly to sugar cultivation, rum production and slave labor. St. Croix's economy existed through trade. The island exported five commodities; sugar, rum, cotton, molasses and hard woods and imported almost everything it needed.

The price of sugar in the world market was stable for the first decades of the 19th century and St. Croix's plantation owners were doing well. In 1803 the population of the island was 30,000 with 26,500 being slaves engaged in planting and processing sugar cane. Prosperity however came to a halt with the closure of Denmark's role in the slave trade. St. Croix had played an important role in the triangular trade route that connected Europe, Africa and the Caribbean in a trade of human cargo, sugar and rum. Around this same time competing beet sugar prices caused a sharp decline in the profitability of cultivating sugarcane. An increasing number of slave revolts motivated governor general of 21 years Peter von Scholten to abolished slavery in the Danish colonies on July 3rd, 1848. With all these factors playing a role St. Croix's economy by the end of the 1820's was nearing ruin.

The late 1800's was a period filled with changes, rebellions and progress. Some of the most famous leaders were Queen Mary, Bodhoe and David Hamilton Jackson. Their efforts and those of other residents were extolled for the good of the local population on issues like improvement of living conditions, freedom of press, education and labor laws.

United States Virgin Islands

In 1917 St. Croix along with the islands of St. John and St. Thomas were purchased by the United States of America from the Danish government for military reasons. In the late 1930's St. Croix's agriculturally based economy was not improving. Economic insecurity continued until the fifties, when tourism became a leading industry in the U.S.V.I.

Today St. Croix is U.S. territory with the main industries being tourism, agriculture and oil refinery. One of the most renowned attractions in the U.S.V.I., the Buck Island National Park is located a short distance from the St. Croix shore. Recently the first casino in the U.S.V.I. was built on St. Croix.

Tourism

St. Croix's history spans the rule of seven nations, each influencing the customs, character, language and architecture of the of the island. Even today, with modern conveniences, St. Croix retains the old world charm that has vanished on many other islands. The pace is slower, and everyone takes time to stop and smell the frangipani!

The island is 1700 miles south of New York, 1100 miles south east of Miami, near the eastern tip of the Caribbean island chain. On the same latitude as Acapulco and Hawaii, just below the Tropic of Cancer, it is eternal summer caressed by cooling tradewinds.

The average temperature is in the mid-80s, and there's just enough rain to keep the ixora, hibiscus and bougainvillea in bloom. The island is 22.7 miles long, and at its widest only 8 miles, but in this stretch there are great varying landscapes. The eastern end is dry, with giant cactus and yucca clusters. The middle is flat fertile land, once the site of massive sugar cane plantations. The western end rises to a height of 1,096 feet on Blue Mountain, culminating in a rain forest of giant mahogany, saman and tibet trees.

The beaches are unique, some quiet coves, some, like Cane Bay, a world renown dive site. Snorkeling is easy, for abundant sea life and coral reefs are close to shore. The high salt content of the Caribbean Sea makes you more bouyant so snorkeling here is easy.

Christiansted: One of two towns on the island, and a National Historic Site, Christiansted was once the Capital of the Danish West Indies, and was founded in

1734. The architectural quality of the town is remarkable, with cobblestone walkways shaded by large arched galleries. The Danes discovered how to adapt 18th Century-style buildings in the West Indies to reduce heat, maximize breeze, and withstand tropical storms.

Trey ceilings let warm air rise in the days before ceiling fans and air conditioning, and cross ventilation is enhanced by rectangular shaped buildings. In fact, even today, many buildings and homes on St. Croix are not air conditioned thanks to this ingenious pratcical design. The buildings were constructed from cut coral blocks (look closely, you'll wonder how they were ever harvested!) and Danish brick brought as ballast.

Thick walls keep the interiors cool, and courtyards and arcades provided shaded retreats. Narrow streets were wide enough for the mule carts of the 1800s! This area, once prestigious residences and mercantile shops of the wealthy Danes, today forms the shopping and restaurant district. Ongoing interest continues and plans are underway for the historic restoration of old buildings on the outskirts of town.

Frederiksted: Victorian Gingerbread, wide streets, and a picturesque waterfront the full length of the town make Frederiksted one of the most beautiful in the Caribbean. Freedom City, as it is known, has a rich history. Smugglers and pirates of the mid-1700s necessitated the construction of Fort Frederik in 1752. The city was destroyed by fire in 1758, and rebuilt in the Victorian style of the era.

Time seems to have passed the city by, but the beautiful park, and open air vendors mart comes alive on the days the sleek cruise ships dock at the new pier. On those evenings, Harbour Night turns Strand Street into a festival, with mocko jumbie stilt dancers, steel pan bans, and street vendor offering local food and drink. Navy ships and subs from the US and foreign fleets dock here often for R&R and frequently give tours of the vessels.

Traveling Information

Rival: Because St. Croix is part of the U.S. Virgin Islands, U.S. Citizens traveling to and from the 50 states as well as the territories of the United States do not need a passport when arriving in the U.S. Virgin Islands from the U.S. or returning to the U.S.

Non- U.S. Citizens are generally subject to the same requirements as traveling from the home country to/from any of the 50 states.

Climate: Sunny, year-round temperatures range in the 80's during the day, 70's most nights with summer somewhat warmer. Easterly trade winds blowing gently across the islands keep the humidity low. Most island showers are quick, tropical, over in minutes.

Average annual rainfall is 50 inches with September and October less dry than the winter months. As there are few wells, residents collect rainwater from rooftops into household cisterns. Salt water distillation plants help the supply. Accordingly, water is precious and cost;y so conserve

Time: Atlantic Standard, one hour ahead of Eastern Standard in the winter, same time as Eastern Daylight in the summer.

What to Wear: Island dress is casual, but bathing suits, short shorts and unbuttoned shirts in town or grocery shopping are frowned upon. Boutiques can fill in or add to your holiday wardrobe. Simple cottons are preferred year round. Men seldom wear ties or jackets. Nobody bothers with raincoats, nor is there much call for sweaters, even at night. Wide-brimmed hats, however, are often required sun protectors.

What to Bring: Not a lot (see above). American travelling irons, hair dryers, razors do not require adapters.

Location: St. Croix lies 18 degrees north latitude and 65 degrees west longitude, close enough to the equator so that twilight comes quickly with, almost always, a brilliant sunset. The Virgin Islands are part of the Antilles chain which forms a long curve from the Bahamas near Florida to Trinidad, off the coast of South America. St. Croix is surrounded by the Caribbean Sea.

Virgin Islanders: Virgin Islanders are a friendly people but they are reserved. A smile and "good morning" go a long way to starting the day off right. Everyone speaks English, or a lilting version thereof. Defined linguistically as Creole, commonly called Calypso, it is spoken throughout the West Indies with speech variations from island to island. Creole began in the early days of the slave trade and was influenced by Portuguese, French, Dutch and English mixed with African.

Services & Organizations

Alcoholics Anonymous (for meeting schedule)	776-5283
Al-Anon/ACOA	773-0372
American Red Cross	778-5104
National Park Service	773-1460
St. Croix Environmental Assoc	773-1989
Tourist Information - Frederiksted	772-0357
Tourist Information - Christiansted	773-1404 x 4801
Toll Free, not from mainland	800-372-USVI
U.S. Customs	773-5650
Cruise Ship Arrival Information	772-0357
FBI	773-7922
FBI - after hours (San Juan)	787-754-6000

Libraries

Athalie Petersen Library, Frederiksted	772-0315
Florence Williams Library, Christiansted	773-5715

Historic

St. Croix Landmarks Society	772-0598
Fort Frederik Museum	772-2021
St. George Village Botanical Garden	692-2874

Arts

Caribbean Dance Company	778-8824
Caribbean Museum Center	772-2058
Island Center	778-5271
Pointe Dance Academy	778-0435

Business & Professional

Chamber of Commerce	773-1435
St. Croix Hotel Association	773-7117
St. Croix Hotel Association - Toll Free	800-524-2026

Airlines

American Airlines	800-474-4884
American Eagle	800-433-7300
Cape Air	800-352-0714
Coastal Air	773-6862
Delta	800-221-1212
LIAT	778-9930
Seaborne Airlines Seaplane	773-6442
U.S. Airways	800-622-1015
Vieques Air Link	778-9858

Emergency Numbers

Police, Fire, Ambulance - Land Line	911
Police, Fire, Ambulance - Cell Phone	772-9111
Divers Alert Network	919-684-8111
V.I. Territory Emergency Management (VITEMA)	773-2244
V.I. Search and Rescue	787-729-6770
St. Croix Hospital	778-6311

Accommodations

Accommodations On St. Croix, Virgin Islands

St. Croix the largest of the Virgin Islands, offers island charm! You can find inns, beach front resorts, casual hotels, casino-resort, golf-resorts and villas built among old plantations overlooking the ocean. The island offers escape and adventure. St. Croix invites you to enjoy your island vacation and take in all that it offers; quiet beaches, fabulous diving, biking tours, hiking trails, historical sites, shopping, restaurants, snorkeling and more.

Several quaint inns and hotels are located in close proximity to the two main towns of Frederiksted and Christiansted. This convenient location offers guest easy access to historic sites, shopping, restaurants, beaches and nightlife that is found in the towns. Access to the remainder of the island requires driving.

Featured Accommodations

The Buccaneer

Visit: www.thebuccaneer.com

Contact or Call (800) 255-3881 (340) 712-2100

The Buccaneer is a premier destination resort for golf, tennis, water sports, weddings, honeymoons and family vacations featuring 138 elegant rooms and a new six bedroom villa. All rooms are designed and furnished to be an intimate retreat, reflecting the timeless elegance of The Buccaneer. Each room features a private patio or balcony for maximum enjoyment of our spectacular views. Founded in the 17th century and family-run for generations, St. Croix's Buccaneer is the Caribbean's and Virgin Island's longest running resort. Both historic and modern, the resort blends old world charm with warm hospitality and the amenities expected by today's traveler.

Cruzan Sands Villa

Visit: www.CruzanSands.com

Contact or Call (972) 747-7575

Cruzan Sands Villa on the Beach is a brand new luxury beachfront villa located in the exclusive Estate Salt River on St. Croix. Our sandy beach, located just in front of the villa, is perfect! With 3-4 bedrooms, the villa can sleep 8 comfortably. Our gourmet kitchen offers the best for the chef among you! Our spacious covered wrap around patio, offers magnificent views of the Caribbean Sea. Sun worshipers have a spacious deck on which to lounge by the fresh water swimming pool. If you are looking for a wonderful vacation in paradise, then you have found it here!

Along the shoreline between Christiansted and the eastern end of the island you will find several fabulous island retreats. Beachfront hotels offer relaxation, quiet shimmering white sands call you to pass your time away under a palm tree embracing the slow pace of island living. At luxury resorts you can do yoga in the morning, breakfast on the beach, golf and a massage in the afternoon. Most resorts and hotels offer beach access, swimming pools, tennis and complimentary water sports activities. As you continue east the scenery changes and so does the development. Many wonderful villas and the Virgin Islands' only casino-resort are to be found on the eastern end of St. Croix.

Moving away from the central areas of the island towards the verdant north, accommodations become fewer and diverse. There are; luxury resort with attractive facilities and activities like golf, tennis, restaurants and water sports, eco-accommodation in the forested mountains that allows for enjoying the great outdoors and gorgeous island villas – your home away from home.

Visit St. Croix and you will enjoy wonderful accommodations, spectacular beaches, world-renowned snorkeling and diving and access to a wide assortment of outdoor activities.

Other Accommodations

NAME	TYPE	PHONE
The Palms at Pelican Cove	Inn	(800) 548-4460
Carambola Beach Resort & Spa	Resort	(888) 236-2427
Tamarind Reef Resort	Inn	(800) 619-0014
Divi Carina Bay Resort	Resort	(877) 773-9700
Hibiscus Beach Resort	Resort	(340) 718-4042
Chenay Bay Beach Resort	Resort	(340) 718-2918

| Hotel on the Cay | Resort | (340) 773-2035 |
| King's Alley Hotel | Hotel | (340) 773-0103 |

Nightlife

St. Croix: Nightlife & Entertainment

St. Croix is a big island with a small island feel. The nightlife is made up mainly of eating out at one of the many great local restaurants and then sitting by the bar drinking and meeting people, listening to live music or taking a spin on the open air dance floor in many cases.

You will find several bars around the island: many are in Christiansted. The local nightlife focuses on music, food and good times. Live music is a popular entertainment. There are a few very colorful bars. Crab races are a unique and popular activity and worth attending if you get the chance – it's a very interesting pastime!

St. Croix is home to the Virgin Islands' only casino – so you can try your luck at the tables or slots! The casino also puts on many musical shows for your enjoyment. Other live performances and plays are performed at the Performing Arts Center. During holidays and local events many night activities take place. Visit the Events Calendar for more details.

St. Croix's resorts and hotels are a great place to go out to and have a great time. Many resorts have special Caribbean showcases including beach bbq, shows and buffets where you can meet locals and other visitors, the friendly atmosphere makes for a great time.

Restaurants

Dining On St. Croix, Virgin Islands

Dining out on St. Croix can mean a great beach buffet, Asian cooking island style, seafood platters, Caribbean delicacies, burgers and fries and on and on! There are so many opportunities to wine and dine on St. Croix.

In Christiansted you will find various restaurants. There are several along the wharf overlooking the sparkling blue water, they are great spots to sit and enjoy the breeze with a nice cocktail after eating a fine dinner. Along the main roads in Christiansted you will find many more restaurants, albeit they may not be open air with spectacular views but always-great food.

The Buccaneer

Visit: www.thebuccaneer.com

Contact or Call (340) 712-2100

St Croix's finest dining, both day and night, are at The Buccaneer. Enjoy casual beach side lunches and seasonal dinners at The Mermaid. Experience award-winning fine dining at The Terrace, featuring Chef Dave (formerly of Kendrick's). Sample vintage cocktails, live music and a light fare menu at the Kendrick's Lounge. The Buccaneer is five minutes east of Christiansted. Secure free parking available. 2014 Wine Spectator Award of Excellence. Open daily.

Many of the resorts offer great dining facilities as well; some include Caribbean themed buffets, fine dining, poolside dining, casino and more. If you are staying at one hotel it is acceptable to go to a restaurant at another hotel property should you wish to do so. Many beachfront properties have beachfront dining, always a gorgeous settings to have lunch and dinner in.

St. Croix is a big island, compared to its sister islands, and there are quite a few restaurants outside of Christiansted and resorts. In and around Frederiksted there are several fun casual dining spots. Other casual local spots are located along the roadside heading east and along the north shore.

St. Croix offers a wide variety of mouth-watering delights.

Shopping

Shopping on St. Croix

Shopping areas on St. Croix include shops, restaurants, bars, attractions and even beaches all in close proximity! The main shopping areas are in Christiansted and Frederiksted. Both towns are historically important to St. Croix and contain numerous historical buildings. Shops are either housed in or near to historic sites. Restaurants and bars are available along the main streets and on the harbor front. Beaches are either a short walk or a very short ferry ride away.

VItraders.com

Visit: www.vitraders.com

Contact or Call (340) 774-1181

You can shop online for your favorite souvenirs, travel guides and maps from the Virgin Islands. VItraders.com has been serving customers for over 14 years. Planning a vacation and need a guide book, beach guide, map or bird watching book? VItraders.com has a great book section. Are you looking for souvenirs like wall calendars, cook books, Caribbean dolls, coloring books, hot sauce, magnets, postcards, mugs, Christmas Cards and ornaments, hats or shot glasses? You will find a nice selection of all of those and more. Click over to VItraders.com for Virgin Islands Books and Souvenirs.

Shopping in Christiansted

You could easily spend the whole day in Christiansted; have breakfast in a cozy cafÃ© while you talk to locals or read the paper. After having your OJ and bagel, head out for bargains and unique Crucian souvenirs. Quaint pavilions and alleys are filled with shops that offer china, crystal, arts, perfumes, clothing, alcohol, jewelry and souvenirs. Small stores often feature unique locally crafted items like hand painted shirts, pottery, bath products, hand made jewelry with island themes, crucian bracelets and crucian rum! After a few hours of shopping take a break and explore the colonial architecture of the historical buildings like Fort Christiansvaern and the Scale House.

The National Park Service that maintains the Fort and other historical buildings has a small store that sells books about St. Croix history; another similar store is the St. Croix Landmark Society. After sightseeing, head for some lunch on the boardwalk and enjoy the pleasant breezes and view. Then its back to shopping for those items you saw and wanted to think about and have now decided you just must have.

In Christiansted the main shopping area is along King Street. Company and Strand Street also offer a variety of fine shops with a large assortment of items. Make sure to explore the small alleys that run between streets and you will discover a mixture of boutiques, many selling unique souvenirs. More shopping opportunities await just east of Christiansted at the Gallows Bay Marketplace, where you will find gift-shops, bookstores, boutiques and other shops.

Shopping in Frederiksted

Frederiksted is also historically significant to St. Croix and contains numerous buildings worth exploring including Fort Frederik. Stores in Frederiksted offer souvenirs and locally crafted items. Frederiksted is not as busy as it was a few years ago, however government and local groups are working on renovating the town and restoring it to its former glory. A few great water sports shops are located in Frederiksted, along with pleasant restaurants and bars.

Shopping Around the Island

Other shopping areas on St. Croix include SunnyIsle and Sunshine Mall which primarily cater to residents and offer pharmacies, grocery stores, clothing stores, movie theatre and offices. Many resorts offer on-site shopping at small boutiques that sell an assortment of souvenirs, clothing, sunglasses, arts and other items.

Shopping on St. Croix offers the convenient ability to sightsee, dine and shop all in one. Shoppers can find crystal, jewelry, perfume, cosmetics, liquor and cigarettes at great prices. Many shops showcase locally made arts, crafts, woodwork, leather goods, ceramics and fabric designs. Be sure to pick up some of these locally made items – they make unique souvenirs. Happy Shopping!

Transportation

St. Croix: Transportation

St. Croix is twenty-eight miles in length and a little over 6 miles at the widest point. St. Croix scenery is beautiful and quiet diverse. There is much to see and appreciate. Travelers may choose from a variety of transportation options; buses, car rentals, limos, taxis, bicycles, scooters, walking, horseback. Your best bet for exploring the island is to rent a car and drive yourself around or to take a taxi tour.

Car Rental Information and Agencies

Renting a car will allow you to see the island at your own pace. There are several agencies to choose from. Car rental agencies have a variety of vehicles; jeeps and cars to eight passenger vans. Renting a car is highly recommended if you plan to spend several days on the island. See information and List of Agencies on Car rental page

Taxi Service Information

Taxi Service is easy to use on St. Croix. Popular spots like the airport and cruise ship pier always have taxis waiting to assist you. Taxis can be called to pick you up at other destinations. Taxis charge per person by destination, there are no metered taxis. See more Information on Taxi Service page

Public Transportation System

The Vitran Public Bus System services various areas of the island. Air-conditioned buses run between Christiansted and Frederiksted about every 2 hours daily from 5:30 am and 9pm. No service on Sundays. They start at Tide Village, to Christiansted and travel along Route 75 to Golden Rock shopping center. They then make their way to Route 70 with stops at Sunny Isle Shopping Center, La Reine Shopping Center, St. George's Botanical Gardens and Whim Plantation before getting to Frederiksted. Bus service is also available at the airport to Christiansted and Frederiksted. The fare is $1 a person. Senior Citizens receive a discounted fare of $.55. The Bus System is not very reliable, if you are limited in time it is not recommendable.

Air Travel

Virgin Islands Inter-Island Airlines

Traveling within the Virgin Islands, Puerto Rico and neighboring Caribbean islands is easy with the use of our professional inter island carriers. Visit St. Croix from St. Thomas in minutes. Fly to Puerto Rico from the US mainland and make a connection from Puerto Rico to St. Thomas or to St. Croix; flight takes 18 to 40 minutes depending on destination. Virgin Gorda in the British Virgin Islands from St. Thomas in only 20 minutes.

As more and more national airlines increase travel from major air transport hubs in the United States, travel to St. Croix is becoming easier than ever. The airport on the island is the Henry E Rohlsen Airport

(HERA), which is located just six miles outside of the town of Christiansted. Its features include a 181 thousand square foot terminal and a 10,004 foot asphalt runway which can accommodate jets as large as Boeing 747s. Although the airport mostly serves regional airlines, there are several that fly in from the United States

Monday throuhgh Friday, Seaborne Airlines offers thirteen roundtrip flights between St. Croix and St. Thomas. Flights start as early as 6:00 am from St. Croix to St. Thomas and then go as lats as 6:00 pm from St. Thomas to St. Croix. All flights are operated on 14-seat DHC-6-300 Twin Otter seaplanes with two pilots and two engines.

Caribbean Buzz Helicopters

Visit: www.caribbean-buzz.com

Contact or Call (340) 775-7335 (347) 284-6335

See twice the islands in half the time! Soar over

mountains, follow the shore line, see sights most visitors never see! Take an exhilarating half hour helicopter tour of the U.S. and British Virgin Islands and all the cays in between. Fly 'doors off' for an adrenaline spiked, wind in your face, one-of-a-kind adventure. Or, take a private excursion to another island! You'll get the same VIP treatment as Eva Longoria, Kate Winslet, Mark Sanchez or Sir Richard Branson. Imagine the thrill of exchanging vows on a secluded beach! Give us a buzz to arrange your tour, day trip or island transfer. FAA approved; 50 years safe aviation experience.

Cape Air

Visit: www.capeair.com

Contact or Call (800) CAPEAIR

Day trips to St. Thomas, St. Croix, Vieques, Mayaguez, Tortola, Culebra and Virgin Gorda are a breeze when you fly Cape Air. Enjoy the view, you'll be there in minutes, with over 100 flights a day to choose from.

For connecting flights, our partnerships with major airlines mean less waiting, simpler ticketing, and faster check-thrus. Cape Air, Your Wings in the Caribbean. Book online at www.capeair.com or call us 800-CAPE-AIR (U.S).

GO2 Charters

Visit: www.go2charters.com

Contact or

Whether you are vacationing, day-tripping, or relocating to the Caribbean, GO2 Charters has a solution for you. We are committed to providing our clients with superior customer service and a personalized approach to air travel. Having trouble moving with your beloved pet with the restrictions of the major airlines? Ask about our ShareFlight Program - a cost-saving way to travel safely and conveniently with your furry friend right by your side. Whether it's a day excursion to paradises like Anegada or Vieques, an aerial tour, or a transfer to the BVI, GO2 Charters will arrange the most appropriate and cost-effective aircraft to fit your needs. Email us for more information.

Air service from the USVI is available to islands throughout the Caribbean. Enjoy your vacation by visiting multiple islands!

Car Rentals

St. Croix: Car Rentals

Exploring St. Croix is best managed by renting a car or jeep. St. Croix is a large island with many beaches and areas of interest. If you would like to explore the island at your leisure the best way to do it is by having your own mode of transportation. Many rental agencies are conveniently located at the airport, at hotels and resorts and in the main towns.

Average prices on rental cars range from $38 to $70 a day. A mid-size four door would run around $38 to $42 depending on season/time of year. A jeep around $45 to $60, an SUV between $60 to $70. Trucks and vans are also available. Special packages are common, so it is possible to get lower prices.

Renting a car will allow you to see the island at your own pace. There are several agencies to choose from. Car rental agencies have a variety of vehicles; jeeps and cars to eight passenger min vans. Renting a car is highly recommended if you plan to spend several days on the island. Having your own transportation will make sightseeing, beach hopping, dining, shopping much more convenient. Enjoy your trip to St. Croix!!

Taxis & Rates

St. Croix: Taxis & Rates

Taxis are a popular transportation choice for visitors to St. Croix. While there isn't a standard type of taxi vehicle, the most popular are vans, open air safaris (converted trucks; truck beds are customized with bench seating in an open-air covered area) and SUVs/cars. Taxis on St. Croix are not metered; rates are per person and per destination and are set by the VI Taxicab Division. **Taxi Rate Sheets** are provided below.

Taxi Tips

➢ Taxis are almost always available at the cruise ship dock when ships are in port, at the airport, the Seaplane Terminal, at the taxi stand area in down town Christiansted and usually at large hotels and popular restaurants/bars.

➢ Licensed taxi vehicles are labeled with: a taxi placard or dome light on the roof, license plates that indicate Taxi status, On Duty/Off Duty sign in the window of the vehicle and a sign, usually on the fender, indicating passenger capacity. The drivers personal identification/taxi license should be on the vehicles dash board.

➢ There are drivers that run "gypsy taxis" in their personal vehicles. They do not adhere to the rules of the taxi commission and are use at your own risk. They often hustle outside bars and grocery stores.

➢ Although rates are standardized it is strongly recommended that you speak to the driver and agree to your total rate (for you, your group, your luggage, waiting, tour) before boarding the taxi.

➢ See the **Special Provisions Section** after the rate sheets for sightseeing tour rates, luggage rates, private taxi rates and other information.

Taxi Rates

AIRPORT TO/FROM:	1 OR 2 PEOPLE	3+ / EACH

Annaly	20.00	10.00
Belvedere	20.00	10.00
Buccaneer	20.00	10.00
Cannan	18.00	9.00
Carmen's Ridge	22.00	11.00
Cane Bay Plantation	20.00	10.00
Cane Garden	15.00	8.00
Carambola	20.00	10.00
Castle Nugent	18.00	9.00
Chenay Bay	21.00	11.00
Christiansted	16.00	9.00
Coakley Bay	22.00	11.00
Constitution Hill	15.00	8.00
Cotton Groove	24.00	11.00
Cotton Valley	24.00	11.00
Cramer's Park	24.00	11.00

Divi Carina Bay	24.00	12.00
Farsham	20.00	10.00
Frederiksted	12.00	6.00
Gentle Winds	17.00	9.00
Grapetree Bay	24.00	11.00
Great Pond	20.00	10.00
Green Cay	22.00	11.00
Ham's Bay/Clover Crest	20.00	10.00
Ham's Bay/Clover Guard	20.00	10.00
HOVENSA	12.00	6.00
Humbug	15.00	8.00
King Frederik Hotel	12.00	6.00
La Grange	15.00	8.00
La Grange HIll	18.00	9.00
Longford	16.00	8.00
Lowry Hill	18.00	9.00

Mt. Washington (East end)	18.00	9.00
Mt. Washington (West)	20.00	10.00
Oxford	20.00	10.00
Petronella	18.00	9.00
Queen's Quarter	15.00	8.00
Selly's Fancy	18.00	9.00
Sandy Point	15.00	8.00
Sandy Point (Nature Conserve)	18.00	9.00
Salt River	17.00	9.00
Seven Hills	20.00	11.00
Shoy's Estate	20.00	10.00
Sion Valley	15.00	8.00
Solitude	21.00	11.00
Sprat Hall	17.00	9.00
St. Croix by The Sea	15.00	8.00
Sugar Hill Estate	16.00	8.00

Sunny Isle	12.00	6.00
Tamarind Reef	21.00	11.00
Tide Village	17.00	9.00
Work and Rest	15.00	8.00
CHRISTIANSTED TO/FROM:	1 OR 2 PEOPLE	3+ / EACH
Annaly	26.00	13.00
Anne's Hope	8.00	4.00
Bethlehem (Upper/Lower)	15.00	8.00
Buccaneer Hotel	9.00	5.00
Boezberg	10.00	5.00
Cane Bay	24.00	11.00
Carambola	30.00	12.00
Castle Coakley/Sion Farm	12.00	6.00
Castle Nugent	15.00	8.00
Catherine's Rest	12.00	6.00
Club St. Croix	8.00	4.00

Coakley Bay	15.00	8.00
Constitution Hill	10.00	5.00
Cormorant	10.00	5.00
Cotton Grove	17.00	9.00
Cotton Valley	17.00	9.00
Cramer's Park	18.00	9.00
Divi Carina Bay	18.00	9.00
Farsham	15.00	8.00
Frederiksted	24.00	11.00
Gallows' Bay	6.00	3.00
Gentle Wind	22.00	11.00
Glynn	12.00	6.00
Golden Rock Shopping Center	8.00	4.00
Grange	8.00	4.00
Grapetree Bay	18.00	9.00
Great Pond	15.00	8.00

Green Cay	12.00	6.00
Grove Place	20.00	10.00
HOVENSAI	12.00	6.00
Hibiscus Beach Hotel	10.00	5.00
Humbug	12.00	6.00
Kingshill	14.00	7.00
La Grande Princess	10.00	5.00
La Reine	14.00	7.00
Longlord	15.00	8.00
Lowry Hill	11.00	6.00
Mon Bijou	14.00	7.00
Morning Star	12.00	6.00
Mount Washington (East)	15.00	8.00
Pearl	12.00	6.00
Peter's Rest	11.00	6.00
Petronella	15.00	8.00

Rust-Up-Twist	24.00	12.00
Sally's Fancy	15.00	8.00
Salt River	22.00	11.00
Seven Hills	16.00	8.00
Shoy's Estate	10.00	5.00
Solitude	15.00	8.00
Southgate/Tipperary	12.00	6.00
Strawberry/Barren Spot	12.00	6.00
Sunny Isle Shopping Center	12.00	6.00
Tamarind Reef	12.00	6.00
Tide Village	8.00	4.00
Upper and Lower Love	18.00	9.00
William's Delight	20.00	10.00
Welcome Estate	6.00	3.00
FREDERIKSTED TO/FROM:	1 OR 2 PEOPLE	3+ / EACH
Annaly	17.00	9.00

Butler's Bay	11.00	6.00
Carambola	27.00	11.00
Christiansted	24.00	11.00
Diamond/St. George's	10.00	5.00
Davis Bay	27.00	11.00
Divi Carina Bay	36.00	18.00
Groove Place Village	15.00	8.00
Groove Place Hills	20.00	9.00
Hannah's Rest	8.00	4.00
HOVENSA	20.00	10.00
Jolly Hill	11.00	6.00
La Grange	8.00	4.00
Little La Grange	10.00	5.00
Manning's Bay	12.00	6.00
Mon Bijou	20.00	10.00
Mt. Pleasant	15.00	8.00

	1 OR 2 PEOPLE	3+ / EACH
Mt. Washington (Frederiksted)	15.00	8.00
Seven Hills	29.00	12.00
Sion Farm	20.00	10.00
Sprat Hall	10.00	5.00
St Croix Renaissance Park	17.00	9.00
Sunny Isle	20.00	10.00
Sunset Beach	6.00	3.00
Whim Plantation/Good Hope	9.00	5.00

CAROMBOLA TO/FROM:	1 OR 2 PEOPLE	3+ / EACH
Buccaneer	32.00	16.00
Chenay Bay	32.00	15.00
Coakley Bay	32.00	15.00
Divi Carina Bay	36.00	15.00
Grapetree Bay	36.00	15.00
Sprat Hall	27.00	12.00
Reef Condominiums	34.00	15.00

Frederiksted	27.00	11.00
Tamarind Reef	32.00	15.00

Special Provisions for Taxi Operators

➤ The charges to areas not listed in the above schedule shall be arrived at by using the nearest tariffed place crossed and the next tariffed place ahead, based on one nearest to the passenger's destination.

➤ A taxi operator, while on duty, shall not refuse any passenger unless the passenger is intoxicated and disorderly, or in possession of a pet or animal (other than a seeing eye dog) that is not properly secured in a kennel case or other suitable container. There shall be no extra charge for seeing-eye dogs.

- ➢ Kennel Charges: Large Kennel – $30, Small Kennel – $20.

- ➢ Round trip fares: double the one-way fare plus waiting charges.

- ➢ Waiting charges $1.00 per minute. First five minutes free.

- ➢ Radio/Phone Call: the fare plus one third of the basic fare.

- ➢ Between midnight and 6:00am, there shall be an additional charge of $2.00 per person.

- ➢ Any one requesting a taxi exclusively for themselves shall pay the rate for four (4) passengers.

- ➢ Luggage: A flat rate of $2 per bag shall be added to the fare for each passenger. The rate for items greater than 30"x20" shall not exceed $4 per item.

➢ Hourly Rates (1-4 Passengers): Sedan/Mini Can: $40, Van/Safari (14 passenger capacity) $55, Safari: $80. Rates for additional passengers will be negotiated between the taxi operator and passengers.

➢ All passengers must be discharged at their precise requested locations when fare is accepted and agreed to.

➢ Sightseeing Tours: One to four people $100, five or more $20 each. Limited time of tour: 3 hours.

Sailing and Boating

Sailing and Boating Near St. Croix

It makes sense that because St. Croix is an island, sailing would be a popular activity for tourists when they arrive, but actually sailing to this destination is just as popular. Whether you own your own watercraft, or charter a crewed yacht, there are tons of accommodations around St. Croix for those who choose to sail to the island rather than fly.

Boat Trips and Day Sailing

Sightseeing, snorkeling, dinner cruises, and even wedding parties are possible aboard the boats that sail around St. Croix on a daily basis. A small number of tour operators exists that specialize in boating and water activities, so if you'd like to spend some time sailing without captaining the boat yourself, you can absolutely make it happen.

If you're just wanting to enjoy some time on the water, without the stress and cost of sailing on your own you should take a day sailing excursion. Wondering what's included and where you'll go? Take a look at the listing that follows for contact phone numbers for area day sailing companies.

BOAT EXCURSIONS

Name	Phone	Location
Big Beard's Adventure Tours	(340) 773-4482	Hotel Caravelle - Downtown Christiansted
Bilinda Charters	(340) 514-2270	Downtown Christiansted
Jolly Roger Charters	(340) 513-2508	Christiansted Boardwalk - Downtown Christiansted
Roseway Sailing	(340) 626-7877	Gallow Bay Dock - Christiansted

Seriously considering chartering a vessel? The following table indicates how to reach a local charter company.

CHARTER AND RENTAL SERVICES			
Name	Phone	Location	Island
Buck Island Charter	(340) 718-3161	Green Cay Marina - The vicinity of St. Croix	
Lady Jasmyn	(603) 781-	3280 Golden Rock - 1.3 mi. (2.1 km) West-Northwest of	St.

Charters	9864	Christiansted	Croix
Llewellyn's Charter	(340) 773-9027	6.6 mi. (10.7 km) East of Christiansted	St. Croix
VIP Sail and Power Yacht Charters	(340) 776-1510	Compass Point Marina - East End	St. Croix

Docking

Sailors will find docking privileges around St. Croix at *Christiansted Harbor, Frederiksted Harbour, Chenay Bay, Cottongarden Bay, Salt River Marina, and Teague Bay.*

Do you plan to travel to St. Croix using your own vessel, or one you charter? See the chart that follows to find basic information for nearby marinas.

MARINAS		
Name	Phone	Location

Green Cay Marina	(340) 718-1453	Tamarind Reef Hotel - 2.4 mi. (3.9 km) East-Northeast of Christiansted
Jones Maritime Dock Marina	(866) 609-2930	Downtown Christiansted
Salt River Marina	--	Clairmont
Silver Bay Dock Marina	--	Downtown Christiansted
St. Croix Marine	(340) 773-0289	Christiansted
St. Croix Yacht Club	(340) 773-9531	6.7 mi. (10.7 km) East of Christiansted

Sailors should note, however, that restrictions do exist regarding sailing the waters around the National Park. You can contact the National Park Service at 340-773-1460 for details. On a final note, if you'll be sailing through U.S. Virgin Island waters for more than six months at a time, you will need to register your vessel with the Department of Planning and Natural

Resources. They can be reaches at 340-772-1955, and are also available to answer any of your questions regarding mooring sites and permits.

NEARBY ANCHORAGES		
Location	Latitude	Longitude
Christiansted Harbor - Downtown Christiansted	17.7486307362	-64.7050631046
Salt River Bay National Historic Park and Ecological Preserve - 4.1 mi. (6.6 km) West-Northwest of Christiansted	17.7746851892	-64.7581708431
Chenay Bay - 3.1 mi. (4.9 km) East-Northeast of Christiansted	17.7611179762	-64.6587789059
Turtle Beach - Buck Island	17.7860968649	-64.6279120445
Teague Bay - 6.7 mi. (10.7 km) East of Christiansted	17.7562455281	-64.6021413797
Cottongarden Bay - 7.8 mi. (12.6 km) East of Christiansted	17.7605164931	-64.5845514536

Frederiksted Harbour - Frederiksted	17.7119103678	- 64.8869007826

However, you choose to make it happen, getting out and doing a little sailing during your time on St. Croix is a must

Activities Guide

St. Croix: Activities Guide

St. Croix offers lots of activities to keep you busy everyday of your trip. You can kayak in the area Christopher Columbus visited in 1493 or go under the sea scuba diving on the famous Wall, get pampered with massages or spend the day exploring the National Parks. Visit the **Beach Guide**, **Attractions** and **Shopping** for more information on these activities.

Day Charters

Enjoying the magnificent waters around St. Croix will be the highlight of your vacation. Sail or motor into quiet coves, snorkel beautiful reefs and just bask in the delightfully warm sun and tropical breezes. A visit to Buck Island is a must! Or take a sunset sail and enjoy the tranquil beauty and romance of Caribbean evenings.

Fishing

Some 21 world records in fishing have been set in recent years in the Virgin Islands; evidence of the amazing experiences that are in store for anglers! Take an offshore fishing charter and test your luck at catching a marlin or enjoy a few hours of inshore fishing for snook and bonefish.

Scuba Diving

Explore corals and gorgonian forest of sea fans. Swim among turtles, parrotfish, blue tangs and so much more. Dive operators are familiar with the various dive locations and can safely guide you to and around them.

They can take you out for the first time, teach you to dive, get you certified and instruct you for higher levels of dive certification.

Turtle Watching
Several beaches on St. Croix are turtle nesting beaches. The St. Croix Environmental Association and other environmental groups monitor these beaches and turtle activity to protect and preserve these beautiful and fascinating marine animals. Environmental groups offer turtle watches and educational trips at various times during the year; some of these trips are limited to members.

Golf & Tennis
The Virgin Islands is home to four golf courses, three of which are located on St. Croix. Tennis courts are available at most island resorts.

Casino/Gaming
The only casino in the U.S. Virgin Islands is located on St. Croix.

Other Activities

Culture/Local Events

Culture in the Virgin Islands is Caribbean meets American, so plan on enjoying it by taking in a local event, trying local food or listening to a local band perform. You might plan your visit around Carnival or during the Jump Ups.

Eco-Tours & Park Adventures

Explore the wonderful natural environment around St. Croix by taking a guided kayak, hiking or snorkeling adventure trip into ecologically fascinating areas. Tours typically include a guide that describes history, ecology and fauna as you go along. A popular area for eco-tours on St. Croix is Salt River.

Horseback

To truly appreciate the "rain forest" on St. Croix a leisure horseback ride is superb. Your guide will introduce you to rain-forest flora and fauna, St. Croix folklore and history. Experienced and inexperienced riders, adults and children are welcome. Prices for horseback tours start at around $50 per person. Beach rides are also available.

Island Hopping

The Virgin Islands (USVI and BVI) are made up of more than 120 islands and cays. There are eight inhabited islands, four in the U.S. Virgin Islands and four in the British Virgin Islands. Each island has it's own unique atmosphere. Ferry service and inter-island air travel makes island hopping possible.

Island Tours

St. Croix is known for its beautiful vistas, historic buildings, scenic drives and just gorgeous scenery. How you take it all in is up to you. The most popular option is an island tour by taxi, but you can also take a walking tour of the historical sites or how about an aerial tour. St. Croix has two distinct landscapes, tall green forest on one end of the island and dry, windswept scrub and grasslands on the other. A scenic drive enables you to appreciate the vast differences in the scenery. The Heritage Trail, a 72-mile driving tour, connects historic sites and attractions and includes many significant natural areas.

Kayak Rentals

Kayak rentals are available at some beach resorts and provide an invigorating way to explore the beach and coastline.

Scuba Diving

St. Croix: Scuba Diving

St. Croix is a great Caribbean destination for scuba diving. Nowhere else in the Caribbean can you dive coral reefs, wrecks, walls and a pier – all in one day if you like! St. Croix offers variety and there is something for everyone; beginner, intermediate and advanced. The underwater world is stunning! Colorful fish dart around the coral reefs and forests of sea fans and sea whips, while other marine animals hide in caverns and under ledges. Observe turtles, bright parrotfish, blue tangs, queen triggerfish, moray eels and so much more.

Starting on the West End of St. Croix are various coral reefs stretching from Sandy Point National Wildlife Refuge north to Frederiksted where you'll find a phenomenal dive at the Frederiksted Pier. The Pier offers impressive diving by day and is fascinating for night dives. The pillars under the pier are home to a variety of soft and hard corals in various colors. It is known for an assortment of unique marine life including the rare batfish, frogfish and seahorses. It is also home to moray eels, octopus, scorpion fish and parrotfish. The colorful corals and unique marine life make the Pier a favorite for underwater photographers and it is considered one of the top macro dives around. North of the Pier are several wreck dives. Wrecks form artificial reefs as they become encrusted in coral and attract fish and other marine life. They are considered particular cool since their former life floating on the sea and their new life beneath the sea offer mystery, history and beauty.

Turning the corner from the West End is the north shore and it offers dive sites from Hams Bluff across to Buck Island, a National Park. These sites include coral reefs, canyons and the renowned wall. 'The Wall' is an area just a quarter mile from shore that slowly slopes then drops thousands of feet, it runs almost the length of the north shore of St. Croix. Various wall dives are available; the most famous is the Cane Bay Wall dive. Another popular wall dive is at the Salt River Canyon.

Dive operators on St. Croix generally offer three trips a day; one or two tank dives in the morning, one or two tank dives in the afternoon and a night dive. Introduction classes, certification and specialty classes are offered. You can start the academic part of your certification online while at home and then finish the open water part while on vacation; going this route means you spend your vacation in the water rather than studying! Some dive operators have discounted accommodations/diving packages arranged with hotels and inns. If you are visiting by cruise ship you will be pleased to know that cruise ships dock in Frederiksted and in walking distance there are dive operators ready to take you out diving.

Wondering what diving in St. Croix will run you? A 2 tank morning dive goes for around $110, and a 1 tank in the afternoon around $70. Night dives are also available. Packages for 3 to 7 days of diving are available; they range in price from $300 for 3-2 tank dives to $475 for 7-2 tank dives. A discover scuba class will be about $70 for shore dive and $120 for boat dive. Certification courses are around $375. Visit our featured dive operator(s) for more information and to book a dive!

Charter Boats

St. Croix: Fishing & Boat Charters

Fishing Charters

Imagine the thrill of going out on a fishing charter while vacationing on St. Croix. You see the captain sizing up a cluster of seabirds on the horizon. You see the birds too, and as you get closer you see splashing in the water. Are the birds circling bonitos and jacks that have been pushed to the surface by...Marlin, Sailfish or Tuna? These gamefish, along with Dolphin Fish (Mahi-Mahi) and Wahoo are what you might hope to catch while offshore fishing. And if it's inshore fishing that interest you, then you can try your luck getting a bite and reeling in some Kingfish, Barracuda, Bonito, Jacks or Yellowtail Snapper.

You might be wondering when the best time of the year is to come to St. Croix to fish! Some species are around all year and others have peak seasons. Fishing charter operators and captains are knowledgeable about the islands' waters and seasons. They can provide information on what you might find on the end of your line when you go out fishing with them during your St. Croix vacation.

Fishing charters in St. Croix include inshore, offshore and marlin trips. Most operators offer trips lasting: 4 hours, typically between 8am and noon, or 1pm and 5pm; 6 hours; 8 hours; and Marlin trips (10-12 hours. Shorter trips are generally inshore fishing only. Boat capacity of 3 to 6 passengers is common. Rates for fishing charters varies depending on length of trip, size of boat, inclusion of fuel in the rate versus fuel being a surcharge, and differences in services and equipment provided. Fishing charters generally have the details of their trips listed on their websites or can provide the information by email or telephone upon request. Explore your options; book a fishing trip and a have a great time!

Did you hope to bring home dinner from your fishing trip? Guests can generally request some of their catch, for example up to 20 lbs, the remainder stays with the boat. If you are interested in taking some of your catch back to your vacation rental to cook up for dinner be sure to ask about it. If you are staying in a hotel you can ask the captain for suggestions of restaurants close to the marina that will cook your catch for you!

If you are an avid fisher you might consider planning your vacation to St. Croix around a fishing tournament, to be a spectator or to participate! Some fishing charters are available for tournaments. A sample of tournaments include: Golden Hook Challenge (February), Dolphin Tournament (March), Guy/Gal Reel Challenge (September) and Wahoooo Tournament (November).

For more information on fish species caught around the Virgin Islands including location, season and bait read from the Virgin Islands Fishing Guide page and for regulations read from VI Fishing Regulations page

Boat Charters

Going on a charter is often the highlight of a Caribbean vacation. Enjoy the wonderful weather, beautiful waters and the service of professional and knowledgeable captains and crew. Charters from St. Croix often go to Buck Island National Monument, an underwater natural monument that offers spectacular diving and snorkeling. Charters are either 6-packs holding a maximum of 6 passengers or larger vessels that can accommodate larger groups or that take several groups out together. Charters are available in ½ day, full day and sunset trips. Prices range from about $60-$95 a person for a full day and $40-$60 for a half day on a group charter. Private charters can be arranged just for your group; prices are around $450-$600. Sunset sails are around $30 per person on a group charter and private sunset sails around $300+, the amount varying by size of boat and number of passengers. Lunch is often included in full day charters. Amenities vary depending on boat.

Virgin Islands: Fishing Guide (This is Virgin Island Fishing Guide related to all Virgin Islands)

Various world records in fishing have been set in the Virgin Islands including the still-standing IGFA Women's 'All-Tackle' world record for blue marlin; a 1073 pounder reeled in by Annette Maudi Dallimor on July 6, 1982. These historic catches, some 21 records over the years, are a testament to the great fishing opportunities that exist in the Virgin Islands for anglers of all ages and experience levels.

Fishing Grounds

The Virgin Islands are perched at the edge of the six mile deep Puerto Rico Trench, an area known for having some of the hardiest game fish in the world. Two well known fishing areas off of St. Thomas are the North Drop, about 20 miles north of St. Thomas; and the South Drop, 8 miles south of St. Thomas. St. Croix is surrounded by a drop which is .5 to 4 miles north or south. Migrating schools of small fish gather in these areas, and this attracts larger pelagics such as billfish, Tuna, Wahoo and Dolphin fish (Mahi-Mahi). "Working the drop" consists of trolling back and forth across the 50-100 fathom depth contour.

Classic flats fishing are a rarity in the Virgin Islands; though exceptions such as the Leinster Bay area on St. John do exist. On St. Croix, which has a narrow underwater shelf off its shores; fishing from small boats very close to the shoreline can be very rewarding. Some recreational fishers have success fishing from shore despite difficulties due to windy conditions, deep drop offs and coral snags.

Offshore Game Fishing

Offshore game fish include Blue and White Marlin, Sailfish, Yellowfin Tuna and Wahoo among others. Most of these game fish strike with little warning and they are all known to give quite a fight. Marlin will fight for hours and are said to become more aggressive the week before and after the full moon. Tuna are also strong fish. Wahoo are known to attack bait ferociously and then swim away from the boat; they can race up to 50 miles an hour!

GAMEFISH	LOCATION	SEASON	BAIT/LURES
Atlantic Blue Marlin	STT North & South Drop, STX 100 Fathom drop off, FADs	All year, best May-October	Lures, Ballyhoo, Belly strips, Mackerel
White Marlin	STT North & South Drop, STX 100 Fathom drop off, FADs	All year, best April-May	Lures, Ballyhoo, Bellystrips

Sailfish	STT North & South Drop, STX 100 Fathom drop off	October-March	Lures, Ballyhoo, Bellystrips
Yellowfin Tuna	STT North & South Drop, STX 100 Fathom drop off and all shelf areas, FADs	August – February	Lures, Ballyhoo Feathers
Blackfin Tuna	shelf areas on all islands, FADs	All Year	Lures, Feathers
Skipjack Tuna	shelf areas on all islands, FADs	All Year	Lures, Ballyhoo
Dolphin Fish (mahi-mahi)	STT North & South Drop, shelf areas on all islands, FADs	October-January (peak season) May, July	Lures, Ballyhoo, Flying Fish
Wahoo	shelf areas on all islands, FADs	All year, best September-May	Lures, Ballyhoo

Inshore Game Fishing

Inshore game fishing is the mainstay of recreational fishing for visitors and residents alike and is a tradition in the Virgin Islands. Inshore game fish include Barracuda, Bonefish, Kingfish, Mackerel, Snook and Tarpon. Methods for inshore fishing include fly rod, top water bait and trolling. Bonefish are a bit trickier to catch as they hide around corals making for an easy snag of your hook/line.

GAMEFISH	LOCATION	SEASON	BAIT/LURES
Bonito (Little Tunny)	most inshore areas, drop-offs and around schools of bait fish	All year, best January-May	Fry, feathers
Barracuda	reef & bank areas	All Year	Lures, spoons, ballyhoo
Hardnose	most inshore areas and around schools of bait fish and FADs	April-September	Fry, small feathers
Bar Jack	most inshore areas and around schools	All Year	Fry, squid, ballyhoo,

	of bait fish		feathers
Crevalle Jack	STX 100 Fathom drop off, most inshore areas and around schools of bait fish	All Year	Fry, squid
Rainbow Runner	STT North and South Drops, reefs & banks, FADs	April – September	Fry, squid, ballyhoo, feathers
Yellowtail Snapper	near reefs & bank areas	All Year	Fry, cut bait
Kingfish	reefs, most mid-shelf areas and drop-offs	All year, best February-May	Ballyhoo, fry, skirts
Cero	Near shore, reefs	All Year	Lures, feathers, fry, ballyhoo

The primary target of shallow water fishing and flat fishing in the Virgin Islands include Barracuda, Jacks and Permit. Bonefish and Tarpon are also popular catches in shallow waters, but they are catch and release only. Snook are caught occasionally.

GAMEFISH	LOCATION	SEASON	BAIT/LURES	FLY FISHING
Bonefish	near shore, shallow areas, sea grass & sand flats, bays, mangrove lagoons	All year, best late March-September	Live shrimp, small jigs often baited with shrimp or crab	Small flies tied to imitate shrimp, crabs
Permit	shallow sea grass & sand flats, bays, lagoons, back reefs	All year, best April-October	Small live crabs, pieces of crab, small sea urchins	Crab patterns
Tarpon	mangrove lagoons, bays, harbors, deeper water	All year, best March-October	Silver spoons, white jigs, live bait fish	Large streamers, various 'tarpon' flies

	adjacent to shallow flats, around offshore cays			
Barracuda	around reefs, channels adjacent to shallow water, mangrove lagoons and bays	All Year	Live fish, bait fish imitations, silver spoons, feathers	Bait fish imitations, needlefish imitations
Jacks	around reefs, channels adjacent to shallow water, mangrove lagoons and bays, back	All Year	Squid, shrimp, cut bait, small spoons, spinners, jigs	Small streamers, shrimp imitations

	reef flats			
Snook	mangrove lagoons, bays, harbors, along beaches with sharp drop-offs and submerged structures	All Year	Live shrimp, small fish, bait fish imitation lures, jigs	Bait fish imitations
Mahogany Snapper	around reefs, channels, adjacent to shallow water	All Year	Batifish, squid, fry	

Regulations

Fishing in the U.S. Virgin Islands is regulated by both territorial and federal restrictions regarding fishing licenses, protected areas where fishing is limited or not allowed, protected species, size restrictions, catch restrictions and other rules that seek to manage fisheries and protect their sustainability. Visit Recreational Fishing Regulations page for more information.

Fishing Events

Avid fishers take note; there are several fishing tournaments in the Virgin Islands throughout the year! Come join in the fun as a spectator or as a participant!

ST. THOMAS	ST. CROIX
Couples Tournament (February)	Golden Hook Challenge (February)
Dolphin Derby (April)	Dolphin Tournament (March)
Memorial Day (May)	Guy/Gal Reel Challenge (September)
July Open Kids Tournament (July)	Wahoooo Tournament (November)
July Open Marlin Tournament (July)	
Bastille Day Kingfish Tournament (July)	
USVI Open/Atlantic Blue Marlin Tournament (August)	

Wahoo Windup (November)	

Virgin Islands: Fishing Regulations (This is Virgin Island Fishing Regulations related to all Virgin Islands)

The waters around the Virgin Islands are home to a great abundance of marine life. Various regulations regarding protected areas, species, size and catch limits are in place to help manage and protect the fisheries. Some of these territorial and federal restrictions are presented below, along with resources for more comprehensive information.

License

General recreational fishing permits are presently not required for recreational fishers in Virgin Islands. This includes persons who engage in fishing for the sole purpose of providing food for themselves or their families and those who catch and release fish. Sale of catch by recreational fishers is not allowed. Recreational fishers cannot use the following fishing gear: pots, traps, set-nets and haul seines.

Recreational fishers however are required to have permits to fish in three special locations: 1. A recreational shrimp fishing permit is required for the harvesting of shrimp from Altona Lagoon and Great Pond on St. Croix. 2. A permit is required to collect baitfish with a cast net within 50 feet of the shoreline or fish with a hook and line in the St. James Reserve. All other fishing and harvest of other animals and plants is prohibited in this area. 3. A permit is required to collect baitfish using only a cast net within 50 feet of the north and south shorelines of Cas Cay in the Casy Cay/Mangrove Lagoon Marine Reserves off of St. Thomas. All other fishing and harvest of other animals and plants is prohibited in this area. Permits can be purchased at the Division of Environmental Enforcement.

Note Commercial fishers are required to have a commercial fishing permit.

Note The British Virgin Islands and Puerto Rico have their own laws and regulations pertaining to fishing. For example, licenses are required for recreational fishing within the British Virgin Islands.

Fishing Regulations: (This is not a comprehensive list.)

➢ Sea Turtles are endangered species. No harvest, no possession and no harassment of sea turtles or their eggs.

➢ Goliath Grouper (Jewfish) is an endangered species. Harvest is prohibited, no possession allowed.

➢ The possession of Nassau grouper is prohibited year round in the territory until the CFMC has determined that it has recovered.

➢ It is illegal to spear fish for lobsters in all Territorial waters. Lobster is to be captured only by hand, snare or trap.

➢ No person is permitted to retain, remove, possess, or injure any conch that is less than nine inches in length from the spire to the distal end, or that has a lip thickness that is less than 3/8 inch. There is no sale of undersized conch shells or meat from undersized conch.

➢ All conchs landed in the Regulatory Area or coastal waters must be alive and intact (in shell) when brought to island on which conch is first sold or consumed. Taking conch to off shore cays and islands for purpose of removing from shell is prohibited. No disposal of shell at sea before landing.

➢ There are various Marine Reserves around the Virgin Islands in which fishing is prohibited, limited and/or require special permits. Contact the Division of Environmental Enforcement for an up-to-date list.

➢ Federal Permit Needed for Atlantic Blue Marlin, White Marlin, Sailfish, Yellowfin Tuna and Skipjack Tuna.

➢ In National Park waters fishing using rod and reel, handline, traps and baitfish nets is permitted. There are however restrictions on gear such as trap size and net size. The use and possession of spearfishing equipment within the park is prohibited. Fishing is allowed outside of swim areas, but not in Trunk Bay and Jumbie Bay on St. John. There are three area fishing closures within the V.I. National Park: A. between 8am and 5pm at the NPS Red Hook Dock and NPS Cruz Bay Finger Pier and Bulkhead, B. within all boat exclusion areas, and C. from any NPS mooring balls. For up-to-date information on fishing regulations within the Virgin Islands National Park, contact the NPS office on St. John at (340) 776-6201 x 254.

SPECIES	SIZE & LANDING RESTRICTIONS	TERRITORIAL WATERS	FEDERAL WATERS	NATIONAL PARK	CLOSED SEASON
Whelk	Minimum size of shell must be great than 2-7/16" in diameter. Must land whole in shell.			1 gal. per fisher per day	April 1-September 30
Conch	Minimum size 9" shell length from spire to distal end, or 3/8" lip thickness. Must land whole in	6 per day per recreational fisher, not to exceed 24 per boat per day.	3 per day per fisher, not to exceed 12 per boat. No use of	2 per fisher per day	July 1 – Sept. 30

	shell.		hookah gear.		
Spiny Lobster	3.5 inch carapace. Must landed whole. No harvest of females with eggs. No spearfishing, hooks or gigs or use of chemicals.			2 per fisher per day	
Yellowtail Snapper			Size Limit is a total length of 12 inches.		
Blue Marlin	No commercial harvest; no sale. Minimum size regulation of 99" Lower Jaw Fork Length.				
White Marlin	No commercial harvest; no sale. Minimum size regulation of 66" Lower Jaw Fork Length.				
Sailfish	63 "No commercial harvest; no sale. Minimum size regulation of 63" Lower Jaw Fork Length.				
Yellowfin Tuna	Minimum legal harvest size 27" fork length and a recreational bag limit of 3 YellowfinTuna per person per day.				

Note Territorial Waters extend from shore to 3 miles offshore

Note Federal Waters extend from 3 to 200 nautical miles offshore.

Golf & Tennis

St. Croix: Golf & Tennis

Golf

The Virgin Islands are home to four golf courses, one of which is located on St. Thomas. There are no golf courses on St. John or Water Island.

St. Croix – Carambola Golf Course

Carambola Golf Course was built by Laurence Rockefeller and designed by legendary golf course architect Robert Trent Jones. The par-72 course winds through a deep valley. Bright tropical plants, tall palm trees and small lakes make the course very attractive as rolling terrain, wind and some 100 bunkers make for a stern test of golfing skill. Although the course can be quite challenging it does provide options for all skill levels to enjoy. The facilities include a clubhouse, practice putting green, driving range and pro shop. For more information, call (340)778-5638.

St. Croix – Buccaneer Golf Course

The Buccaneer golf course, designed by Bob Joyce, is an 18-hole course that sprawls across much of the resort's 340 acres. From the hilltop buildings all the way down to the shoreline this course is beautiful and known as one of the most scenic on St. Croix. The attractive site is also very challenging with a par-70 course encompassing 5,810 yards worth of fairways, bunkers and water hazards. Recent renovations include the addition of a three-hole walking course, water station and landscaping improvements.

Buccaneer Golf Course is open to the public. There is a fully stocked pro shop. Tee times should be scheduled at least two days in advance. Golfers may play until sunset. Motorized two-person carts are available and walking the course is permitted.

St. Croix – The Reef Golf Course

The Reef is for those golfers less inclined to take on the more challenging 18-hole courses or those looking for a more casual game. The Reef Golf Course, located in Teague Bay, offers nine holes of enjoyable golf. The course spans some 3,100 yards of beautifully maintained fairways and greens. Nestled in a valley below The Reef Villas on the north-eastern end of St. Croix, the course offers a good golfer a moderate challenge, while its open layout also allows beginners to enjoy the game. Both riding and pull carts are available for an additional fee. For more information, call (340) 773-8844.

RESORT/CONDO PROPERTIES FACILITIES	PUBLIC COURTS FACILITIES
The Buccaneer Resort	

Carambola Beach Resort	
Chenay Bay	
Club St. Croix	
The Reef	
Tamarind Reef Hotel	

Virgin Islands Culture (This is Virgin Island Culture related to all Virgin Islands)

Caribbean and American, that is a description of culture in the United States Virgin Islands.

You will find fast-food restaurants like Subway and McDonalds next to local restaurants serving pates and boiled fish. You will find large grocery stores selling everything from Campbells Soup to Sara-lee pound cakes. Around the corner from the grocery store will be a fisherman selling a fresh catch from his truck. On the radio you can hear calypso music, reggae, American pop, salsa, blues, oldies, rock and roll and many other genres. Florida oranges and strawberries are sold as are kenips, mangos and coconuts. Fashions include jeans, t-shirts, jerseys, polo shirts and other Western style dress. Local sports enthusiast watch and play baseball, basketball and football. And CNN news is broadcasted daily and discussed just as often as local gossip. Together the American and Caribbean combination makes the United States Virgin Islands a unique and interesting place.

The population in the USVI is largely made up of Caribbean people whose ancestors were Africans and Europeans. You will find people from all across the Caribbean living in the Virgin Islands as well as Americans from the mainland, Europeans and Hispanics.

English is the main language in the USVI and the majority of the population speak, write and read English only. Some residents speak quickly and with an accent making it difficult to understand. Emigrants from other islands have brought other languages to the Virgin Islands therefore it is not uncommon to hear Spanish, French-Patois and Creole.

Music in the Virgin Islands is definitely Caribbean. You can hear reggae, steel pan, calypso and soca. Many other music venues can be enjoyed from Latin and blues to jazz and classical.

Virgin Islanders are religious people. Popular religions include Baptist and Catholic.

Superstitions and storytelling are very common. There are often stories about jumbies (spirits) that walk around in homes, on the street and anywhere the person telling the story wants them to be. Jumbie stories are a Caribbean tradition and are often used as cautionary tales for children. Bru Nansi, a spidery-man who prevails in the most adverse circumstance, is a popular story character.

In the Virgin Islands saying Good Morning, Good Afternoon and Good Night are not the same thing as saying Hello or Hi; the former is a warmer greeting and is the norm for friends and strangers.

While visiting the islands take your time to appreciate the local arts, events and music. Definitely try some local food, deserts and drinks, you will enjoy them. Make your vacation a true Caribbean experience by enjoying the local culture!

Island Terms

Mocko Jumbies: Colorfully costumed stilt dancers, like the one in the picture above. They can be seen at carnival parades and other local events. The word jumbie refers to ghost-like spirits of West African belief.

Quelbe: Is a style of music and dance. The musical sounds that are danced to are made by scratching instruments made of hollowed out gourds. The band is called a scratch band.

Kenips: Are a type of fruit. They have a green outer shell and a fleshy edible meat around a large seed inside.

Virgin Islands Language

The official and most widely spoken language in the Virgin Islands is English. The literacy rate in the Virgin Islands is around 90-95%.

It is common to hear French Creole and Spanish spoken, particularly on St. Thomas and St. Croix. Spanish is spoken in the Virgin Islands by immigrants of Puerto Rico and Santo Domingo. French Creole is spoken by immigrants from St. Barthelemy, St. Lucia,

St. Martin, Dominica, French Guyana, Guadeloupe, Haiti and Martinique.

While English is the official language and widely spoken it is often spoken with an accent and rapidly, therefore some words may at first sound unrecognizable to a speaker of standard English. Additionally a Creole English exists and it involves different pronunciations, unique vocabulary and doesn't adhere to many grammatical rules.

Languages Spoken in the Virgin Islands

Population over 5 years of age

LANGUAGE SPOKEN	POPULATION	%	ENGLISH AS 2ND LANGUAGE
English	74,740	74.7%	
Other Language	25,319	25.3%	
Spanish	16,788	16.8%	6,428
French & French	6,578	6.6%	1,673

Creole			
Other Indo-European	1,043	1%	223
Asian & Pacific Islands	262	.3%	83
Census: 2000, US Census Bureau			

Language History

While English is the dominant language today this was not always the case, and its dominance can be considered comparatively recent. The most popular languages spoken within the past 400 years in what is today the US Virgin Islands are English, Virgin Islands Creole English and Dutch Creole.

The US Virgin Islands became a United States territory and official English speaking region in 1917. The islands were formerly the Danish West Indies. During the 245 years of Danish ownership the official language was

Danish, however it was never established as the common language. Today it is not part of language in the Virgin Islands with the exception of Danish street names in historic areas.

Many settlers on St. Thomas, between 1665 and the early 1700's, were Dutch. The general population in those days was an array of people who spoke many languages including Danish, Irish, Dutch, Scottish, English, Spanish and French. The African slaves that were imported to the islands came from different tribes and countries and they also brought their own native languages. Within individual social circles mother tongues were spoken. To communicate with everyone in the community residents had to learn bits and pieces of other languages. What developed from this borrowing from here and there was a Creole language. As a majority of the initial settlers were Dutch, the language that developed was a Dutch Creole.

Dutch Creole included some Dutch, Danish, English, African, French and Spanish words. Spanish words were primarily for animals and fruits. French words retained were often verbs. The Dutch Creole language that formed is known as 'Negerhollands' and it was generally used by slaves amongst themselves. Planters learned the language in order to communicate with the slaves and later the general population shared this language.

In the middle of the 1700's Moravian missionaries sought to bring Christianity to the slave communities in the Danish West Indies. Initially sermons and classes were strictly oral and in Dutch Creole, however the missionaries gradually added books. The New Testament translated into Dutch Creole, for example. As the Creole language alone was too basic to translate such works, words from the standard Dutch language were utilized, thus creating an almost new Creole or blended Dutch Creole. This blended Dutch Creole was considered artificial as compared to what was spoken in the colloquial language.

Lutheran church services for the black population were held in Creole until the 1830's.

During the early 1800's a linguistic change had begun; English became more prevalent. Encouraging the move to English was British occupation in the islands between 1807 and 1814. Instruction for children attending confirmation classes were in English with Dutch Creole as a foreign language. Additionally, English had long been the popular choice for business in Charlotte Amalie's busy trading port. By the early 1880's Dutch Creole could be heard only among a few older people. The Dutch Creole language is today extinct in the Virgin Islands. There is little written material of the colloquial language and the religious texts that were translated were heavily blended with Dutch.

St. Croix was owned by the French until 1733 when the Danes bought it. By 1741 there were 5 times as many English on the island as Danes. English Creole emerged on St. Croix more so than Dutch Creole, which was more popular on St. Thomas and St. John. A dialect of English Creole called Cruzan is heard on St. Croix today.

Creole languages are simple with little use of grammar. Consequently even when the shift from Dutch Creole to English occurred there was still great difficultly in much of the populous with correct forms and grammar. An English Creole formed as the populous learned English verbs, nouns and adjectives but lacked the correct rules for putting them together. Phrases beginning with "I is" and "I be" illustrate the lack of grammar rules. Such phrases can still be heard today; often in casual conversations between locals and particularly between children.

Virgin Islands Creole English is described by some linguist as a transitional language, a bridge between Dutch Creole and standard English. Virgin Islands Creole English overlapped for some time with Dutch Creole. The last native Dutch Creole speaker died in 1987. Virgin Islands Creole English was common in the early 1900's and up to the 1970's. Today many of the words are still used, however standard English is the most widely spoken.

A characteristic of Creole English that is still very popular is the doubling of words as a way of reinforcement. For example one might say 'good good' in response to 'how are you'. Also, there are a wealth of proverbs, like 'poor people must not have warm hearts' and 'monkey know which tree to climb'. These proverbs are still widely used in the Virgin Islands.

Creole English is seen as 'bad English' and is often associated with the poor and uneducated, therefore parents and teachers often criticize and correct children when they use Creole English rather then standard American English. Most older children and adults in the Virgin Islands can quickly switch between Creole English and standard English when having a conversation.

Examples of Virgin Islands English Creole

WORD	MEANING
Dem	A way of pluralizing a noun. 2+ cats would be "the cat dem".
Bomba	an overbearing person.
Bambola	a lively dance to a distinctive drum beat.
Bamboshay	a lively dance.
Gongolo	a species of millipede.
Ganga Man	a herbalist.
Nana	a nurse who cares for small children.
Yaya	a pet name given to a woman in the Virgin Islands in

	former times.
Kunu-munu	a man who has become foolish because of excessive love for a woman.
Mumu	a stupid person.
Bamacoo	a hernia.
Kallalloo	a dish made of leaves, meat and fish.
'Nyampe	mucus in the corner of the eye.
Ponko-lonko	a term of endearment used to a small child, and of contempt used to adults.

Virgin Islands People

People from the Virgin Islands are called Virgin Islanders and based on the island of residence are called St. Thomian, St. Johnian, Crucian and Water Islanders respectively.

The first people known to have inhabited what is today the Virgin Islands were the Carib, Arawak and Ciboney

Indians. These indigenous people are believed to have left and/or been forcibly removed by the late 1500's.

Between the early 1600s and mid-1800's the residents of the islands were of European and African extraction. Settlers, mainly from Holland, England, Denmark, Ireland and France, came to the islands to operate plantations, to run shops and warehouses, as indentured servants and to live in the fledging new colonies. Outnumbering the European whites were African slaves that were forcibly brought to the islands as labor for the plantations. Whites and Blacks born in the islands were called Creoles. At the end of the plantation era many of the white planters and their families returned to Europe.

In 1917 the United States bought the Virgin Islands from Denmark. The population in the late 1800s and throughout the 1900s changed greatly. There was an influx of immigrants from neighboring Puerto Rico to

St. Croix to work in agriculture. French immigrants from St. Barths and British immigrants from the British Virgin Islands came to St. Thomas and today are well established. As a new US territory American officials and military personal were sent to the islands. These five groups made up the majority of the population in the early 1900s. After Naval rule ended most of the military personal and officials returned to the mainland and a new group of US mainlanders began coming to the islands; tourist! With tourism came a boom in the economy and another influx of immigrants. This was the mid-1900s. More French from St. Barths and more British from the British Virgin Islands came to work in hotels and restaurants on St. Thomas. Americans from the mainland came to the islands to invest in hotels and property and to enjoy island living. As tourism grew and the prospect of better jobs and a better livelihood so did the population. Large numbers of immigrants from throughout the Caribbean came to the islands and while this migration is much smaller today it still continues. Presently almost every island in the Caribbean is represented in the Virgin Islands from St. Kitts to Trinidad and Dominca to Anguilla.

A small close knit Middle Eastern community established themselves in the Virgin Islands shortly after the 1967 war in which Israel occupied areas on the west bank of the Jordan river.

There is also a small but well established Indian community in the Virgin Islands, mostly on St. Thomas. The Indian community is made up primarily of Sindhis.

Today the population of the Virgin Islands is 78% black, 10% white and 12% other. While 81% of the population is of West Indian background only 49% were born in the Virgin Islands. The remaining 32% were born elsewhere in the Caribbean. Residents originally from the US Mainland make up 13% of the population and Puerto Ricans make up 4%. The remaining 2% is a mixture of immigrants from across the world including the middle east, India and Asia. (Source: US Census Bureau – 2000)

While the population of the Virgin Islands may seem largely the same and residents may outwardly express nationalistic pride as Americans and Virgin Islanders, residents do not forget where they and their neighbors are from. A Virgin Islander will quickly differentiate themselves from other residents who are from neighboring Caribbean islands. Differentiations are also made between white Virgin Islanders from old families, from French families and white continentals. Differences between residents from St. Kitts, Dominica, Trinidad, Puerto Rico, Haiti, Santo Domingo, Tortola... are not forgotten and most residents can identify the various groups by differences in accent, slight differences in skin color and facial features and last names. While the population is largely Black West Indian, it is still an ensemble of different groups.

Virgin Islands Music

In the Caribbean, African rhythms were fused with European elements creating new Creole musical forms that continue to develop into unique musical expressions today.

In the Virgin Islands you can hear Caribbean rhythms, intoxicating steel drums, high-energy dance music, spiritual hymns, soca, reggae, blues, salsa, meringue, jazz, classical and an assortment of other music genres. While a variety of music types are played in the Virgin Islands, it is calypso, soca, reggae and steel pan beats that are the sounds of the Caribbean must often heard.

Calypso

Historically, calypso music can be traced to the days of slavery. It was a means of communication and a vent to the strains of oppression. Calypso has it's roots on the island of Trinidad. Present in Trinidad during French and Spanish occupation, calypso did not take root until

English occupation. With English as the common language Calypso could now be understood by the entire population. Calypsonians are respected as news carriers and what they sing is considered to be truthful interpretations. Calypso is most famously known for expressing political commentary through satire and sarcasm. Today Calypso has evolved into two types, the traditional informative Calypso and a new dance hall type of calypso music.

Soca Music

Add some soul to Calypso and you have Soca. The origin of the music is Trinidad and Tobago. The lyrics are used to express political and social commentary.

Reggae

Reggae music is an offshoot of ska music. The order of creation is ska then rock-steady then reggae. Famous reggae artists like Bob Marley, Peter Tosh and Bunny Wailer began their careers as ska musicians. Ska music started as dance music. Audiences wanted a more steady beat, and the music evolved into the more mellow reggae of today. Reggae lyrics usually have an emphasis on redemption. Reggae music has traveled and become popular across the world.

Other Caribbean music types that can be heard in the Virgin Islands

Fungi: Is a musical form native to the British Virgin Islands. It is characterized by a variety of instruments and is sometimes called a scratch band.

Meringue: Is a high energy music characteristic of islands such as Puerto Rico and the Dominican Republic.

Rock Steady: Is the precursor of reggae. It is slower, heavier and more vocal.

Salsa: Is a Latin dance music developed in Puerto Rican and Cuban communities in New York.

Zouk: Is a dance music from the French Antilles and is played in both slow and fast beats.

Popular Musical Events in the Virgin Islands
Various music venues occur throughout the year. During Carnival there are often Latin venues, Calypso Shows, Steel Pan performances and other musical showcases. Blues festivals, jazz concerts, reggae concerts, steel pan shows, zouk music and more are sponsored at hotels, at restaurants and at local events.

Virgin Islands Food & Drinks

Food and drinks are an important part of Virgin Island's culture. Every festival, party, graduation, birth, wedding or holiday celebration must have food! Local foods in the Virgin Islands include an assortment of Caribbean dishes. It is common to find American dishes, restaurants with various cuisines and fast food restaurants in the Virgin Islands.

Drinks

Rum, rum and more rum! Throughout the Caribbean, every major island has its own varieties of rum. Rum is distilled directly from sugar cane or molasses. As such rum was originally manufactured along side sugar on sugar plantations in the Caribbean. Today the Virgin Islands are well known for Cruzan Rum, manufactured on St. Croix.

There are a number of popular health and fruit drinks common to the Virgin Islands and the Caribbean. Seamoss is a popular drink made of seaweed that is boiled until it dissolves and then mixed with milk and spices. Mauby is made by boiling mauby bark with spices including cinnamon and is a local favorite. Other favorites include; passionfruit juice, pumpkin punch, sorrel, soursop punch, banana punch, coconut water, peanut punch, bush tea and lemon tea among others.

Caribbean Food

The foods common to the Virgin Islands today and to the Caribbean are a result of interactions between the indigenous Indians and Europeans during the early years of exploration in the Caribbean region, Europeans and Africans during years of colonization and through interactions between immigrants from neighboring islands and Americans in more recent times.

The first known inhabitants of the Caribbean region were Indians and from them European settlers gained knowledge of local fruits and vegetables. The Indians raised ground provisions like cassava and knew how to make bread from it. While most of the indigenous Indian cuisine has not survived, their influence is still apparent. One of the enduring cooking methods the Indians used was barbecue!

In the early days of colonization in the Caribbean two groups with vastly different cooking styles and ingredients lived together; Europeans and Africans. The Europeans brought recipes and food products like beef, onions, garlic and wheat that were unknown to the region. They also brought many food items that are today synonymous with the islands such as breadfruits, limes, mangos and sugar cane. With the importation of African slaves came new crops like okra and new cooking styles. From the Americas came beans, corn, potatoes and varying types of peppers.

When slavery was abolished many laborers abandoned the fields leaving a need for workers. European nations adopted a system of indentured servants which were often from China and India; the new groups brought more cooking styles to the Caribbean. One dramatic and lasting result of Indian migration to the Caribbean is a spice mixture called curry. Curry dishes have become popular in Caribbean cuisine.

Caribbean cooking has many dishes. The best cooks are often the older women in the community. Asking for a recipe is often pointless as they do not cook with recipes but rather with memory and taste; they add a little of this and a little that and create masterpieces. Fish soup is popular and on some islands it is eaten for breakfast, lunch and/or dinner! Callaloo soup is another popular dish; it is made of leaves from a daheen plant mixed with okra, local herbs and often various meats or seafoods. Stewed oxtail, beef, goat and chicken are all popular. Saltfish is favorite as a dish or in pates. Side dishes include rice and peas, yams, fried plantains, dasheen, sweet potato, cassava, beans and lentils. Below you will find a few recipes for island favorites!

Virgin Islands Recipes

Meat Pate

Directions

Step I. Pastry

- ➤ 4 cups flour

- ➤ 4 level tablespoons unsalted vegetable shortening

- ➤ 1/2 teaspoon salt

- ➤ 1/4 teaspoon baking powder

- ➤ 1 cup water

Mix dry ingredients in large bowl. Cut in shortening with knives or pastry blender. Add water gradually to form a soft dough. Knead gently on a floured board for a few minutes. Cover and let rest for about 10 minutes. Shape into small balls, roll out and cut into size circles desired for turnovers.

Step II. Filling

- ➤ 1/2 lb. lean ground pork AND 1/2 lb. ground beef OR 1 lb. ground beef (omitting pork)

- ➤ 1 large sweet pepper

- ➢ 1 medium onion

- ➢ 1 tablespoon minced celery

- ➢ 1 tablespoon minced parsley

- ➢ 2 tablespoons margarine

- ➢ 1 clove garlic, crushed

- ➢ Hot pepper to taste (optional)

- ➢ 1/4 cut tomato paste

- ➢ 1/4 teaspoon Oregano

- ➢ 1 tablespoon fine bread crumbs

Sauté pork in margarine until brown, usually about 10 minutes, add beef and continue cooking another 5 minutes. Add remaining ingredients. Cook for a few minutes longer (make sure beef is cooked, no longer pink) If filling seems very dry add a little water.

Step III. Prepare and Cook

Place filling on each circle of dough, leaving edge bare, moisten edge with water, turn over and seal meat inside dough by pressing moist edge together with fork. Fry in hot deep fat, until dough in golden brown.

Attractions guide

Attractions on St. Croix, Virgin Islands

St. Croix encompasses 84 square miles of history, beaches, beautiful vistas and culture. The island has many sites to see and enjoy; from wild life reserves and historical towns to underwater marine parks and botanical gardens. Both Christiansted and Frederiksted can be explored on a walking tour or self guided. Outside of town you can take a tour or rent a car and take in the island at your own pace.

St. Croix is rich with historic sites; most are associated with the plantation agriculture that made St. Croix a rich sugar producing island during Danish reign. You can take a driving tour and visit many of beautiful points and buildings of historical importance; like windmills, great houses, plantation villages, schoolhouses and churches. There are many excellent examples of colonial architecture all over the island and you will no doubt see dozens of mills scattered across St. Croix.

St. Croix is the largest of the U.S. Virgin Islands and its topography is very different from it's sister islands. There are large expanses of agricultural flat lands, very mountainous and lush forest and dry grassy plains. Several wildlife and ecological reserves offer you the rare opportunity to see endangered birds, turtles and incredibly diverse marine ecology. Exploring these natural areas is a treasure and will make for a memorable vacation.

With so much to see and do in St. Croix it is a great idea to browse through the photos and descriptions of St.

Croix's attractions and make a plan of the things you would like to visit while vacationing on the island. If you are visiting St. Croix on a cruise your time is more limited, select the attractions and/or beaches you would like to visit in order to make your day on St. Croix rewarding and fulfilling!

Christiansted, St. Croix

Christiansted, the capital of the Danish West Indies from 1755 to 1871, is one of two main towns on St. Croix. Located between a busy seaport and green hillsides, the town is well known for it's many historic yellow buildings. The one square mile town of Christiansted offers you a unique opportunity to visit a historically important town as well as to partake in shopping and dining in a modern setting. Christiansted has maintained it's Danish architectural richness and offers many buildings and structures of interest, like cobblestone walkways, old churches and imposing fort Christiansvaen.

The Christiansted historical area encompasses about 27 acres and is maintained by the United States National Park Service. It is located along the Christiansted waterfront and it includes what used to be a busy Danish business and trading center. It was once the area used to dock ships carrying human cargo, rum and molasses bound for the triangular trade route through the Caribbean to Europe and Africa. Christiansted is a very interesting town and well worth exploring.

Apothecary Museum

This special building was a 19th century Danish colonial pharmacy and is the only Danish pharmacy museum in the Western Hemisphere that exist in its original building. The pharmacy was located in this building from 1828 to 1970. The apothecary was restored by the

St. Croix Landmarks Society and opened in 1996. The pharmacy was established by Peder Eggert Benzon to prepare medicines for the Danish military in Christiansted. The last owner of the pharmacy was Laurence C. Merrill who purchased it in 1946. Merrill continued to operate the pharmacy until he retired in 1970. He donated the contents of the pharmacy including handsome antique drug jars and pharmaceutical equipment to the St. Croix Landmarks Society. The Museum is open Monday through Saturday 10am to 4pm. Admission is free.

Fort Christiansvaern

Constructed in the late 1700s of yellow brick, Fort Christiansvaern is the best preserved of the five Danish forts remaining in the West Indies. The fort is a wonderful example of Danish colonial military architecture. Although built for defense against pirate and privateers as well as to ward off slave uprising, its cannons have never known warfare. The fort is built around a small courtyard and includes corner bastions and small dark dungeons. Originally used by the Danish Army the fort later served as a jail and also for religious services.

Government House

A beautiful example of Danish colonial architecture, Government House illustrates the grandeur of Danish buildings from the period when 'sugar was king' in the West Indies. Government House is an imposing building located on the lower King Street area and is hard to miss. A large welcoming arm staircase graces the entrance of the building and leads up to an arch bearing the date 1830.

This building is one of the largest governor's residences in the Lesser Antilles. Inside are reproductions of the original furniture. These furnishings were a gift from the Danish government who took the originals with them when they left in 1917. In 1871 the capital of the

Danish West Indies was moved to Charlotte Amalie however Government House continued to serve as a government building and today it is the focal point of many government social and cultural events. The building was originally the site of a Danish merchant's home. This home was purchased and merged with another house to form the present government house

Old Scale House

Through the gates photographed here you enter a room will a large scale, thus the name scale house. The scale house saw countless hogheads of sugar pass through in the colonial days. The sugar was weighed and taxed before being shipped to Denmark, America and various European countries. The building was also used to inspect imported goods. Since the beginning of Danish settlement a scale house was part of waterfront trading scenes. This scale house was built between

1855-1856 and is located right on the Christiansted waterfront.

The Steeple Museum

The simple but pretty rectangular building directly across from the Fort's main entrance road was once the Lord God of Sabaoth Church. It was built in the early 1750's by the Danish West India and Guinea Company. The church was consecrated in 1753. The baroque tower and cupola were added about forty years later. The Steeple Building was St. Croix's first Lutheran Church. Later the structure was used as a military bakery, community hall, hospital and also a school. The National Park Service has restored it to its original splendor. The museum contains several displays that portray the history of St. Croix and plantation life.

Old Danish Customs House

The beautiful yellow customs house sits in the lawn in front of the fort. The customs house was the third building in a local chain of commerce. After merchants passed through the scale house on the Christiansted waterfront their next stop was the custom house to pay taxes. The construction of the building reflects both European style and the modifications necessary for island living; for example the welcoming arms staircase graces the front of the building and then the addition of hurricane shutters shows the need to protect the building from the elements. This building dates back to 1734 when it was a single story bookkeeper's residence. Later additions included the second floor.

Frederiksted, St. Croix

Frederiksted is a picturesque water front town. It was established in 1751 and it is the second largest town in St. Croix. It is a lovely historic town that is easily explored in one day. Federiksted is built in a Victorian style; this was the style chosen after the original buildings were destroyed in a fire in 1758. Centuries ago Federiksted competed with Christiansted as a port of trade; Christiansted became the more important of the two. However, Federiksted would also have its day of glory and it's mark in history. The fort at Federiksted fired the first foreign salute in honor of America in 1776. It is still called the Freedom City, a name it earned as an ally to the British colonies that became America.

Emancipation Park (Frederiksted)

The area right in front of the Frederiksted fort and waterfront has been made into a beautiful town park. It contains statues of historically important Virgin Islanders. Small paths weave through dozens of large Mahogany trees and fragrant flowers. This pleasant Frederiksted park honors the slave revolt leader

General Buddhoe and also serves to recall and honor the 1848 proclamation by Governor Peter von Scholten that emancipated slaves in the Danish islands. The park has many benches and a small gazebo.

Fort Frederik

A National Historic Landmark, the red and white Fort Frederik was built in the 1750's to ward off pirates. It is an excellent place to visit and learn about the importance of the U.S.V.I. in world history. In 1776, the first salute from foreign soil to the new nation of the United States of America was fired from the fort. The salute of Old Glory which had been raised on an American brigantine at port in Frederiksted was a violation of the laws of Denmark's neutrality however the islands had helped the British colonist in America sealing a friendliness between the two colonies, and the salute was therefore appropriate. It is from this fort that Danish Governor Peter Von Scholten emancipated the slaves on July 3rd, 1848. The fort includes a museum and art gallery.

Historical Buildings of Frederiksted

There are many historical buildings in Frederiksted that have been converted into offices and stores. The one photographed here is the Customs House on the Frederiksted Waterfront. The customs house is an elegant eighteenth century building. Many other buildings exist including churches and government buildings. You can walk through Frederiksted on a historical tour with a guide, this is the recommended way to learn and appreciate the small town, or you can walk around by yourself. Small shops and restaurants are also located within the mix of historically important buildings.

Nature Reserves on St. Croix

Buck Island Reef National Monument

The Buck Island area was first protected in 1948 and later became a national park in 1962 under the direction of John F. Kennedy. Buck Island National Monument is 6000 feet long and ½ a mile wide. Uninhabited Buck Island is 340 feet above sea level. The National Park Service manages this underwater monument of extraordinary marine beauty.

Buck Island offers a pristine white sand beach; excellent snorkeling and a wonderful look at marine life around spectacular coral reefs and gardens. There are several species of coral and almost 90 species of fish in the park's waters. This 880-acre monument created by nature is a mile off the northeast coast of St. Croix. It is made up of 176 acres of land and 704 acres of underwater area. It is one of the most popular attractions on St. Croix.

The crystal clear water and beautiful underwater scenery at Buck Island is legendary. With a mask and snorkel you will be treated to some of the most fabulous underwater views in the Caribbean. This ecological site may take the whole day to explore. There are hiking trails on the island that are worth visiting and underwater trails to follow while snorkeling. Several species of turtles and birds nest in the area. Two thirds of the island is surrounded by an Elkhorn coral reef and coral gardens. The water is teaming with hundreds of colorful tropical fish. Without question Buck Island is a must see.

Salt River Bay National Historical Park and Ecological Reserve

Salt River Bay is a pristine and beautiful area. Mangrove lagoons, lush forest and waterways are worth a drive to look and enjoy the scenery. Salt River is the only documented site under the U.S. Flag where Christopher Columbus' fleet landed on the voyage of 1493 to the New World. Columbus had spotted a settlement on the shores of Salt River and sent a group to explore and look for potable water. A skirmish ensued between the Caribs and the explorers.

Today the site of Columbus' landing is a National and Territorial Park. Salt River is the site of many ecological and historical treasures. The St. Croix Environmental Association conducts tours, and kayak sightseeing is available. The Salt River Bay National Historical Park and Ecological Preserve encompasses the largest remaining mangrove forest in the USVI.

Beaches

St. Croix Beach Guide

St. Croix's palm lined and sun kissed beaches call visitors to spend a couple hours and sometimes the entire day enjoying the natural beauty. Miles of secluded spots can be found along St. Croix's shores; in fact many beaches on St. Croix are continuous with different segments having different names.

Take a look at the 23 beaches included in this guide and select your favorites – you are certain to find a few!

Cane Bay
Cane Bay is a great spot for sunbathing, walking, snorkeling, having a cool drink at a beach bar or just hanging out. The long white sand beach is lined with many trees which provide good shade. Cane Bay is renowned as an excellent snorkeling and scuba diving site. About 1/4 mile offshore, the depth plunges to 1,000 feet, so divers can merely swim out and dive "the wall", as it is called. This beach is easily accessed from the main road. A dive shop, kayak shop, restaurant & bars are located in walking distance from the beach. Volleyball net is available on the left side of the beach. The water is usually calm but there can be strong currents.

Chenay Beach

Chenay Beach is a pretty little beach. Home to a hotel with the same name, the beach is open to the public. This white sand beach offers both a relaxing atmosphere and beach fun. Wind surfers, snorkeling, kayak and sunfish rentals are available. A beachside bar and restaurant makes you feel far away from everything else and is perfect for lunch and drinks while enjoying the tranquility of the beach. There is some sea grass in the areas close to shore. Swimming out along the right side to the point affords good snorkeling. A children's playset is located just behind the tree line.

Coakley Bay

Coakley Bay is a beautiful white sand beach that is often sparsely populated. The water has a good bit of sea grass in it so often the shoreline will be littered with sea grass. The beach offers views of Buck Island. Coakley Bay offers very good snorkeling. The ocean floor bottom is rocky in some places and these areas are strewn with sea urchins, so beware. Although there are no palm trees on the beach, shade can be found under the sea grape trees. Accessible by a dirt road; a small sign that reads 'Nature Preserve of St. Croix Environmental Association' marks the turn in for the road.

Columbus Landing

Columbus Landing is a small, white sand bay with some pebble filled spots. There is a good shell searching, but remember it is illegal to remove seashells from beaches in the Virgin Islands. The water deepens quickly and has many areas with seagrass. There is limited shade. No development or amenities on site. This beach is historically important; it is the landing place of Christopher Columbus' exploration party during his voyage in 1493. You can walk along the rocks on the right side (when facing the water) to see Salt River a National Park protected area with natural and historical importance.

Cramer's Park

A great beach and very popular with residents. On weekdays the beach might be sparsely populated but on weekends its party central with family picnics, parties, gatherings, sometimes camping and definitely loud music. The water deepens gradually and is usually calm. Camping is allowed and there are sheds, restrooms and other park amenities like picnic tables & grills.

Davis Bay

Davis Bay, a long sandy white beach, is typically quiet and relaxing. The middle of the bay has some rocks and the far left side experiences some mild surf which can be fun for body surfing if the condition are right. The currents can get strong. Coconut palms and other trees are scattered along the shore providing some shade. This beach is a lovely spot to spend a quiet day; the beautiful, undeveloped hills on the far left and the gentle to mild wave action set an atmosphere of being far away from everything. While the beach is quiet there is a resort on the beach, Carambola Resort.

Divi

This lovely white sand beach offers you a relaxing day in the sun. Palm trees line the sandy shoreline. Home to Divi Carina Bay Resort this beach is in easy access to water sports, bar and restaurant and even a casino. You can walk along the Divi Beach to Grapetree Beach which makes for a great beach stroll. Enjoy the pool side bar and restaurant at the Divi. Order a delicious cold tropical drink and sit under a palm tree while enjoying paradise. Fair snorkeling can be enjoyed.

Dorsch (Sandcastle Beach)

Dorsch is a beautiful long beach located a short distance from Frederiksted. The shoreline is mostly sandy but there are a few rocky spots, this is the case in the water as well. Good snorkeling is available around the rocks. On weekdays the beach is quiet. On weekends and holidays it's popular for family picnics and parties. A section of Dorsch is sometimes called Sandcastle Beach due to a hotel on site with a similar name. There are two hotels on the beach and restaurant/bar facilities are available.

Fort Frederik Beach

Frederiksted Beach is walking distance from Frederiksted and the cruise ship pier. A small, lovely white sand beach that offers instant access to the lovely Caribbean Sea right from the Frederiksted waterfront. This beach tends to be heavily populated when cruise ships are in port. Cruise ship passengers can sight see around St. Croix, shop in Frederiksted and then take a relaxing swim before returning to the ship. Popular spot for fishing in the evening and for watching the sunset.

Grapetree Beach

Grapetree Beach is a narrow, long, beautiful white sand beach. It runs along the same stretch as the Divi Beach. The shoreline is perfect for a nice, relaxing day on the beach. A few palm trees can be found on the far end. It makes for a lovely walk. Several residential homes are close by so respect the private property that boundaries this lovely beach. Snorkeling is decent and turtles can sometimes be spotted. This beach is often quiet and makes for a great spot to read, think, picnic and to just unwind.

Isaac Bay

Isaac Bay is long, mostly sandy. The far right is rocky with some sand and sandstone. Short shrubs line the shoreline; they provide little to no shade. The waters are mostly calm with the exception of the rocky area on the right and it deepens quickly. The bay is framed by beautiful, undeveloped hills.

Located on the far eastern end of St. Croix are Jack and Isaac Bays. They include 301-acres (122-hectares) of white sand beaches and upland forests and make up one of the few pristine ecosystems remaining on St. Croix. They are perfect for those looking for an off the beaten track beach. Jack and Issac Bays are accessible by hiking only and are often sparsely populated to unpopulated.

Snorkeling is excellent in the area. Coral reefs in these bays are home to at least 400 species of fish, including parrot fish, blue tangs, four-eyed butterfly fish and sergeant majors. These beaches have the largest nesting populations of green and hawksbill turtles on St. Croix and are under the care of the Nature Conservancy. Beach access may be limited during some periods of turtle nesting season. The Conservancy invites visitors to study turtle behavior and the landscape around Jack and Isaac Bays during guided hikes they conduct in an effort to educate visitors and collect funds to support their turtle monitoring and protection programs. Trails start at Point Udall down past East End Bay; behind the large satellite across from Cramer's Park and up past Goat Hill and from the far left of Grapetree Bay.

Jack's Bay

Jack Bay is mostly sand, small pebbles and seagrass. The tree line is made up of seagrape trees, acacia and grass — limited to no shade. The water deepens more gradually than at Issac and there are reefs within the shallow areas.

Located on the far eastern end of St. Croix are Jack and Isaac Bays. They include 301-acres (122-hectares) of white sand beaches and upland forests and make up one of the few pristine ecosystems remaining on St. Croix. They are perfect for those looking for an off the beaten track beach. Jack and Issac Bays are accessible by hiking only and are often sparsely populated to unpopulated.

Snorkeling is excellent in the area. Coral reefs in these bays are home to at least 400 species of fish, including parrot fish, blue tangs, four-eyed butterfly fish and sergeant majors. These beaches have the largest nesting populations of green and hawksbill turtles on St. Croix and are under the care of the Nature Conservancy. Beach access may be limited during some periods of turtle nesting season. The Conservancy invites visitors to study turtle behavior and the landscape around Jack and Isaac Bays during guided hikes they conduct in an effort to educate visitors and collect funds to support their turtle monitoring and protection programs. Trails start at Point Udall down past East End Bay; behind the large satellite across from Cramer's Park and up past Goat Hill and from the far left of Grapetree Bay.

Manchenil

Manchenil is a very long, white sand beach on the south side of St. Croix. Accessible by a dirt road, look for the pink pillars off South Shore Rd. The beach is usually sparsely populated to unpopulated on weekdays but is popular on weekends. There is limited to no shade. The water is calm and deepens gradually.

Mermaid Beach (at Buccaneer)

Mermaid Beach is a great white sand beach and is home to the Buccaneer Resort. The shore is dotted with many tall, beautiful coconut trees; they provide ample shade for those seeking refuge from the bright Caribbean sun. Some areas of the water are rocky and there are parts with seagrass. Conch and starfish are attracted to seagrass so its possible you might see some of those sea critters along with other marine life. A beach bar and open-air restaurant is located a short distance from the sandy beach front; perfect for getting a bite to eat or a cool drink. The beach is often busy with hotel guests during high-season.

Protestant Cay

Take a short ferry ride over from Christiansted to Protestant Cay, home of Hotel on the Cay. The sandy little beach on Protestant Cay is delightful for sunning and swimming. The water deepens gradually but does open up to the harbor. You can enjoy a stunning view of the Christiansted and Fort Christianvearn from the tranquility of the beach. A few palm trees and palm-covered umbrellas offer shade. (The ferry departs from the boardwalk that is in front of the park next to Fort Christianvearn; it runs from 7am to 6pm and costs $3 round trip.)

Rainbow Beach

Rainbow beach is a small, sandy bay. On the far right and left it gets rocky, however the beach itself is mostly sandy. Limited to no shade. A great little beach bar is located on site and often has live music in the afternoons. A volleyball net is available. Rainbow is very popular on Sundays; on weekdays it is quiet and sparsely populated.

Reef Beach

Reef is a small, quiet beach. The water can be a bit choppy. There are some rocks in the water and many areas with seagrass. It is a popular spot for wind surfing. A few sea grape trees line the shore which is sandy but littered with lots of dried sea grass.

Sandy Point

This 3-mile beach is the longest in the Virgin Islands. It is located at the southwest end of St. Croix, just south of Frederiksted. The vegetation in the area is stunted due to salt stress and the tree line starts much further back from the water than is typical at other beach on St. Croix so shade is not available. The long, wide stretch of bright white sand is an awesome sight. The water deepens very quickly at the beach. The 380-acre Sandy Point peninsula is a protected reserve for leatherback and other sea turtles; it is one of the most important leatherback nesting grounds in the world and hosts the largest nesting population of leatherback sea turtles under United States jurisdiction. The dirt access road is open Saturday and Sunday from 10am-4pm. The beach may be closed during the turtle nesting season from March through August.

Shoy's

Considered one of the prettiest beaches on St. Croix Shoy's has crystal clear water and white sand. A few sea grape trees line the long beach. The beach is quiet and relaxing. The beach is usually sparsely populated on weekdays. Access is available through the guarded, gated entrance on the right when entering Buccaneer Resort; drive past the golf course, residential area and then park in the small parking area; follow the short path to the beach. There is a residential area close by so respect private property boundaries. The east end of the beach is better for swimming while the opposite end offers good snorkeling.

Sprat Hall

This is a pretty bay located a short drive from Frederiksted. The beach is mostly sand with some areas of rocks. The water has a gentle surf and it is rocky close to shore. A nice beachside restaurant & bar is perfect for grabbing a bite to eat and a couple cool drinks.

Tamarind Reef Bay

Tamarind Reef Bay is a nice beach to enjoy a variety of activities; lay out on the beach, sit under one of the palm trees that line the shore, have a tropical cocktail at the poolside bar, have lunch at the restaurant, snorkel, kayak, lay in a hammock and read a book... lots to do and enjoy. The bay is rocky on the far end and swimming is limited to certain areas because of the rocks. Water is shallow in the near shore swimming areas. The shoreline is sandy with pebbles. Seagrass in the water and along the shore is common. There is a marina nearby.

The Grotto (at Buccaneer)

The Grotto is located at the Buccaneer Resort, just one cove over from Mermaid Beach. The Grotto is mostly sandy with a rocky shoreline area. The beach is long and makes for an enjoyable stroll. Chairs, kayaks, restaurant & bar are available at the resort. Hotel guests have free access to the beach.

Wedding Planning

Getting Married on St. Croix, Virgin Islands

Does your dream wedding take place on a secluded beach? How about at sunset with steel pan music playing? Or perhaps on a sailboat! Whatever your tropical dream wedding entails, it can be arranged in the Virgin Islands. Couples that want to exchange their vows in the beautiful USVI will find the islands ideal. Many hotels and resorts have wedding packages that include the wedding arrangements and accommodations. If you want a special location then a wedding coordinator can arrange all the details for you. Ceremonies can be elaborate or simple.

St. Croix
Perhaps your wedding entails horseback riding or an old Danish sugar-mill; look no further then St. Croix. Imagine steel pan music playing softly as the bride arrives, she is beautiful, the scenery is beautiful, the weather, the cake – everything is perfect! You can choose to marry under a floral archway on the beach, in a resort gazebo or in a historic sugar mill. So many options, and after the wedding so many more options for enjoying the honeymoon; diving, quaint beach bars, day trips to Buck Island, shopping and more!

Wedding Consultants

A wedding consultant based in the Virgin Islands is your best resource for planning your wedding. Whether the consultant is affiliated with a hotel or is in private business their knowledge of island weddings will make everything so much easier for you. Hotel packages might run anywhere from $550 up to $3000+. Prices depend on the package and can include the basics; a great location and the minister or can include bouquets, cake, photographer, champagne, limo, crystal flutes, videographer and live music.

The Buccaneer

Visit: www.thebuccaneer.com

Contact or Call (800) 255-3881 (340) 712-2100

Celebrate one of life's most joyous occasions in one of the world's most spectacular settings. Recently featured on ABC's The Bachelor, The Buccaneer offers the romance of the setting sun over a gentle sea, the historic charm of a centuries-old Sugar Mill, the bliss of a flowering garden. Enjoy the ambience - and each other - and let our experienced wedding planners take care of the details. We can accommodate a memorable wedding for just the two of you, as well as a wedding and reception for up to 100 friends and family. Special honeymoon packages are available!

Private consultants can arrange your wedding basically anywhere you choose but often will suggest the areas that are best suited for such an event. Packages can be basic to elaborate with prices around $300 and up. A consultant can take care of everything for you; processing the license, getting a great photographer, flowers, cake, caterers, transportation and if necessary even witnesses! They will insure that your day is extra special, just the way it should be!

The Virgin Islands are perfect for anniversaries and renewing vows! Consultants can plan these events as well and make it extra special for just the two of you or for the whole family. Contact a local wedding consultant and start planning your island dream wedding or vow renewal.

If you are planning to arrange the wedding yourself you will find wedding license information for the USVI below.

Request Marriage License Applications

The marriage license application fee is $200 ($100 for application fee and $100 for the license). There is an 8 day waiting and processing period, which can be waived depending on circumstances. The application is good for 1 year. Court marriages in front of a judge are performed on weekdays by appointment and will cost around $200. Religious ceremonies should be arranged directly with church officials. If either party has been divorced, a certified copy of the divorce decree must be presented. If you are requesting a marriage license through the mail, without the help of a local wedding consultant you will have to pick up the license yourself on arrival. This can only be done of regular business days.

St. Croix
Superior Court of the Virgin Islands

Family Division

P.O. Box 929

Christiansted, St. Croix USVI 00821

Real Estate

Real Estate on St. Croix

St. Croix, the largest of the Virgin Islands, is home to diversification in people, culture, architecture and history. St. Croix's landscape is equally diverse: the topography changes from flat agricultural land to rolling hills; arid areas to lush vegetation; countryside settings to dramatic sea views. Whatever your likes are, there's bound to be an area in St. Croix that appeals to you. The diversity of the island is reflected in the real estate market. Properties of all types can be found on St. Croix including high-end houses, fixer-uppers, condominiums, commercial properties and undeveloped land.

Coldwell Banker St. Croix Realty

Visit: www.coldwellbankervi.com

Contact or Call (340) 718-7000 (340) 778-7000

Your St Croix Real Estate experts, Coldwell Banker St. Croix Realty is a full service agency for both property and home purchases and holiday or long-term rentals. We offer an array of luxury villas, condos, homes and vacant homesites where you can build your dream home in America's Paradise The largest and most rural and residential of the U.S. Virgin Islands, St. Croix covers 84 square miles. There are many varieties of St. Croix property, which can range from a beachfront property to a mountaintop villa or a condo on the harbor, and more. Please contact us by phone, e-mail, or visit Coldwell Banker St. Croix Realty online.

Team San Martin, RE/MAX St Croix

Visit: www.teamsanmartin.com

Contact or Call (340) 773-1048 (340) 690-2934

Why Choose Team San Martin? Market and Industry Knowledge! Joe and Julie have been St Croix real estate innovators since 1984. We know the island, neighborhood by neighborhood. We know where we are going before we take you there. We constantly improve our skills and keep ahead of new marketing and technology strategies. We spend meaningful time with you to identify your needs; and explain the entire process, to avoid surprises along the way. Our relationship does not end at closing; we offer on-going support for all your real estate needs. Your personal real estate advisors! Team San Martin. Teamwork makes Dreams work!

There are presently 271 homes listed that vary from fixer uppers to luxury properties. The price range of houses currently on the market is $39,000 for 1 bedroom, 1 bath aged fixer upper cottage; to 5.9 million for a luxury beach front 8 bedroom, 10.5 bath on a 3.69-acre lot. The $500,000 and upwards price range affords exquisite properties with nicely appointed interiors, spectacular views and ideal locations. These homes make up 34% of the available residential properties. Within this market 43 properties are luxury homes worth $1,000,000+. As would be expected, these homes are worthy of design recognition. Properties in the range of $300,000 to $500,000 are also beautiful homes with views, pools and good neighborhoods. These homes make up 17% of listed properties. The price range of $200,000 to $300,000 yields comfortable homes in good areas, convenient to everything; and they make up 15% of listed properties. Homes under $199,000 are typically modest homes and fixer-uppers. These properties make up 34% of the available residential market.

Many of the residential properties on St. Croix are designed with apartments attached to the main house or detached cottages. The additional income could be a welcomed asset.

Most residents finance their homes through conventional mortgages with local banks. Interest rates are slightly higher in the Virgin Islands than on the mainland. A typical down payment is 20 to 30 percent. Banks require earthquake and windstorm insurance with mortgages; the cost is around 2-3% of replacement value.

The condominium complexes on St. Croix vary in design and location; though all typically have at least one pool and some with tennis courts and restaurants. Each of the complexes has unique amenities whether it is located on a renowned golf course, steps away from a beach, historical ruins on the premises or strategic vantage points for spectacular views.

Currently there are 101 condominiums on the market ranging in price from $30,000 for a 1 bedroom, 1 bath 578 square foot condo in Vista Mar; to $1,395,000 for a luxury 4 bedroom 4 bath 3,240 square foot condo in Coakley Bay. The majority of the condo units are priced at $100,000 to $350,000; these properties make up 68% of the listings. Units priced at $70,000 and below are typically small one bedroom units or studios. For pet lovers, it is good to know that some of the complexes are pet friendly.

Condominiums are often purchased as an investment to be rented as a vacation or long-term rental. Many of the complexes have on-site Property Management companies. In addition, there are independent companies specializing in Property Management as well as Realtors who offer similar services.

The availability of time share (fractional ownership) properties is very limited.

One of St. Croix's largest commodities is vast open space. Much of the land is easily built on and have views; a great combination. There is still ample room for growth without diminishing the natural beauty of the island. Currently there are 546 listings of land available on the market ranging in price from $15,000 for a .32-acre lot in La Grange; to 12.5 million for an 81-acre waterfront estate. A typical .5 acre lot with a view will be approximately $45,000 to $75,000. An acre of land with a view may cost $75,000 to $150,000. While most land sites are less than 1 acre in size large parcels of land of over 60 acres are also available. Presently on the market there are large land sites Including an 40 acre lot and a 101 acre lot.

It is recommended that a relationship be established with a realtor who will in turn be able to assist you with your specific needs. It is always best to visit St. Croix to see firsthand the areas that most appeal to you. The process of purchasing property on island is akin to stateside procedures. There are many local lenders and mortgage companies that will be able to assist in the process.

The real estate market in St. Croix offers a diverse inventory of listings at reasonable prices, contact the featured agents above for more information.